MW01232165

CELEBRATING

YEARS

OF GOD'S FAITHFULNESS
1977-2017

CELEBRATING

40 *YEARS*

OF GOD'S FAITHFULNESS

1977-2017

Compiled and Written by
Marlene Ulrich

Commissioned by
Ephrata Community Church Elders

Ephrata Community
CHURCH

To the faithful congregation of Ephrata Community Church

To the pioneers who paid the price in leaving
what was comfortable to follow the passion of Jesus in their hearts
To those who walked together, served together,
and sowed into the congregation through various seasons
And to the generations that will experience a
supernatural reaping of the harvest in the years to come

May the Lord bless you and keep you and make
His face shine upon you.

To God be all the glory!

CONTENTS

Chapter 4

Building for the Harvest 2000 – 2014

Chapter 5

Passing the Baton 2014 – 2017

Appendixes

PREFACE

Several years ago, Kevin Eshleman, lead pastor of Ephrata Community Church, approached me with the idea of writing a book on the history of the church. ECC was coming up on its 40-year anniversary celebration, and it would be an ideal time to compile the church's history as a reflection of what God built and a look forward to what is yet ahead.

This book is an account of God's faithful leading and intervention in the lives of the people who have belonged to Ephrata Community Church in the past 40 years. It began with a handful of young believers who had a passion in their hearts to unconditionally give everything to follow Christ, never imagining they would grow to a church of 1,400.

I am an eyewitness and participant in this story of God's faithfulness as one of the initial core members. Throughout the years, I have also served in church leadership and worked many years as an administrator in the church office. As I began to review and immerse myself deeper into the history of Ephrata Community Church, I became overwhelmed and at times fell on my knees to worship our God who has so faithfully carried us through the years.

As I considered how best to communicate the past 40-year history of Ephrata Community Church, it became clear in my spirit that it should not consist of only historical dates and events, but rather be told as a narrative, highlighting a God who tenderly cared for and fathered His church. So while there are dates, photos, and people mentioned throughout the book, I trust you will experience the faithful story of God as He carried a small group of teenagers, and those who joined them over the years, into their God-given destiny.

Finally, it is important to recognize that this 40-year history is not about us as people; it is all about Him. In our weakness and frailty, God carried us and did immeasurably more than we could have ever asked or imagined. As we build upon what God has already done, by faith we believe His ever-increasing, victorious Kingdom will continue to advance in saving the lost, healing the sick, and releasing the captives.

I am most grateful for Amy Zook, who spent countless hours editing the manuscript. I thank all those who added their expertise in reviewing and proofreading the manuscript. And a special thanks goes to Kelly Belousov for her professionalism in designing the cover and layout.

I want to acknowledge the eldership team of Ephrata Community Church for the commissioning of this project. They lead with unity and integrity, through which the church inherits an immense blessing.

— Marlene Ulrich

Ephrata Community Church elders from left: Mark & Marlene Ulrich, Jared & Mindi Bruckhart, Barry & Cheryl Wissler, Kevin & Stephanie Eshleman, Kay & Glenn Weaver, Rosene & Ivan Martin, Joanna & Jon Chappell, 2014.

(1)

THE EARLY YEARS: BUILDING A FOUNDATION 1977 – 1981

BIBLE STUDY GROUP

IGNITING A PASSION

In the early 1970s, a group of about eight teenagers began meeting regularly on Wednesday nights as a Bible study in the musty basement of the Fellowship Center of the Ephrata Mennonite Church, located on a side street near downtown Ephrata, Pennsylvania. A fire burned in the hearts of these young people, as they were bent on following after the Lord and desired to live their Christian lives as close to the book of Acts as possible. That zeal, breathed on them by God, was the spark that would ignite a passion within them to relentlessly pursue all that God had for them. Influenced greatly by the Jesus People Movement of that time, these zealous teenagers embraced a new form of fellowship, which accepted all denominations, reached out to the lost, and saw many salvations. They attended Jesus Festivals, held by The Jesus People, in the field of a local farm in nearby Morgantown, Pennsylvania. These meetings provided the group with the energy to emerge from their denominational restraints and brought a new freedom to their religious lives. The Jesus People also introduced the practice of community among believers, which they quickly adopted. Equally influential in the foundation of this group was the local chapter of the Full Gospel Businessmen Fellowship, where the

Bible study group fellowshipping in basement of Glenn and Mildred Wissler's home, ca. 1976.

gospel of Christ was preached, and the ministry and work of the Holy Spirit was taught and received.

Before long, the small group began looking for a more neutral and comfortable environment to meet weekly, and the Bible study moved in 1975 to the home of Glenn and Mildred Wissler. The meetings were originally held in the living room. The group began to attract even more visitors, mostly teenagers. "Contemporary worship," as we know it today, was led by a few novice guitar players, who taught that worship was a way of connecting with God. Young people sat on the wide windowsills, up the open staircase, and anywhere on the floor where there was available space. As numbers swelled into the forties, Glenn and Mildred offered to finish their basement for more space. After cleaning the stone wall, adding homemade furniture, carpeting, and an entry room, the group moved their meetings to the basement. This allowed for drums and a piano to be added to the several guitars already being used for worship. The atmosphere was electric with the manifest presence of the Lord, as the group expressed their praise with the raising of hands and other demonstrations of worship.

The early meetings were initially led by a team of three teenagers and were relatively unstructured. From time to time, outside speakers were invited to come and teach. Other times, the group would simply worship and create an atmosphere where they could encounter God and be changed by Him. Many invited their unsaved friends from school and saw them meet Jesus in sincere repentance.

Genuine worship became one of the foundation stones of the not-yet-established church. Many times, their passionate worship would continue long after a meeting was officially over. Retreats were often filled with hours of music and dancing. On one particular retreat, as the group met on the second floor, they were asked to stop dancing because of the noise on the ceiling below.

EMBRACING THE HOLY SPIRIT

During the 1970s, teaching on the Holy Spirit was a new thing, particularly in the Lancaster County region. Many of the denominational churches were not accepting of the move of the Holy Spirit, so this group of believers became like a watering hole in the desert. Those teenagers who had encountered the Holy Spirit and wanted to follow His leading were the ones who continued to attend the weekly gathering. Their meetings became a time when they would experience and receive things that they couldn't in their own churches. It became a place for these young, passionate Christians to walk out some of the new things of the Spirit. They were taught principles of the Kingdom and what it meant to be "Spirit-led" or "filled with the Spirit." Mark Ulrich reflected back saying, "All those things were new and refreshing, and I actually enjoyed getting together and hearing about God. On top of that was the whole relational aspect. I was a shy, quiet guy, but coming and building relationships just kind of brought you out and gave you more confidence in who God created you to be."

In the midst of these exciting times, without realizing it, a house church was forming. Each week, new youth came from all over the area and from all kinds of different church backgrounds and denominations—Mennonite, Brethren, Lutheran, and Catholic were among them. This was a new move of God in the area, as up to this point most believers did not associate with those from other churches and denominations. It was unique in that there was an acceptance of believers in an atmosphere of unity. Kay Weaver recalls, "For me, it was like coming home. At first, I was nervous coming because I didn't know anybody. But it didn't take long until I just felt so at home, and friendships started. It was a stretch for me with worship. I was baptized in the Holy Spirit at one of the meetings." The room soon became packed, with up to 70 individuals on any given week. Some young married couples began attending in addition to the mostly single crowd. God had begun to gently blow on the spark that he had ignited in this group, and the flame was spreading.

A generation older, Glenn and Mildred Wissler served as hosts to the group. They recount, "Actually, it was fun to watch these kids. We remember one evening, we counted that they were from 13 different churches. They all got along well, and they were all just so excited. They came in the door, threw their coats on a large pile on the sofa, and went down to the basement. It was pretty exciting to watch. There were some pretty neat things happening with the kids. Every week, they would bring new ones along, some with problems, and it was neat to see what was happening." Mildred added, "We didn't always agree with everything. But we knew their hearts, and that's what always kept Glenn and I here." The Wisslers faithfully and graciously remained involved as God was growing this group and spent many hours interceding on their behalf before the Lord.

KOINONIA LIVING

Up to this point, there was no intention of starting a church. These teenagers were just interested in youth ministry, a Bible study, lots of

Bible study group at retreat, ca. 1976.

worship, and teaching. But as they immersed themselves in these things, they discovered that what they were really enjoying was community as described in the book of Acts. They were opening their lives to each other and allowing others to lovingly correct them where they needed to grow. They desired to genuinely love one another. With time, they realized that they wanted to be more intentional in their relationships, to know and support one another in "koinonia living." Koinonia living is a lifestyle in which believers hold all things in service to their brothers and sisters. In other words, it is the helping of each other, the loving of each other, and the giving to each other. This lifestyle is based on the desire to see none lacking in spirit, mind, or body and a willingness to share in a common life, vision, and destiny under the Lordship of Jesus Christ. So in addition to the meetings, they added many more activities like hiking, hayrides, and retreats, all of which more fully developed their friendships. Glenn Wissler added with a smile, "And they always wanted to play volleyball."

As often happens during a new move of God, rumors began to emerge about the worship and what occurred in the basement meetings. While it was a difficult time for the group, they continued to grow, making mistakes in the process. They shared a heart for God and a sense of adventure even in the midst of criticism, which eventually opened doors of opportunity with invitations to speak and hold programs elsewhere.

Women doing yard work together, ca. 1977.

15

Was there a future for this small group of believing teenagers? They were a very young and inexperienced group. What credibility did they have? Many on the outside discussed whether it would last and thought it was only a matter of time until they stopped meeting. One wise older man stated, "Well, if there is commitment, that's what will determine if it will last or not." And there was commitment with this group. They possessed a commitment to follow Jesus Christ together, wherever He would lead them under the power of His Holy Spirit. God was breathing His life into them as they continued to seek Him.

SERVANTS OF LOVE COMMUNITY CHURCH

"They were continually devoting themselves to the Apostles' teaching and to fellowship, to the breaking of bread and to prayer" (Acts 2:42 NASB).

There eventually came a stronger sense among the group that perhaps God was intending to birth a church out of this fellowship. While many were still attending their respective churches, they were seeing these regular meetings as a place where they were receiving more spiritually. Over time, it was becoming like "their church," and so it was a natural move to respond to God's leading and consider establishing themselves as a congregation. The word circulated within the group about forming a church, and plans began to formulate through those early discussions.

A NUCLEUS OF TWELVE
Out of the approximately 70 who attended the Bible study, there were twelve individuals who responded as wanting to "stay and be a part of this new church." Most of the people said, "No, I'm committed to my home church and will attend there." The rest were at a place where they needed to finish commitments at their home churches or needed more time to process their decision. The twelve individuals who initially founded the church were Jay Good, Judy (Martin) Groff, Ray and Janie Martin, Jay Oberholtzer, Mark and Marlene Ulrich, Glenn and Kay Weaver, John Weaver, and Barry and Cheryl Wissler. These twelve were young and

naïve enough to overlook any fears in planting a new church. With the zeal of God in their bones, they felt far more prepared and knowledgeable than they really were. As a group with an average age of 20, they had a whole lot of faith and not a lot to lose. They had a commitment to each other and a real sense of family, which made the decision to follow the Lord and form the church somewhat easier.

With the nucleus of twelve, the new church met for the first time on October 16, 1977, in a living room at one of their homes. Leadership naturally fell to a team of three leaders: Ray Martin, John Weaver, and Barry Wissler. The God-given entrepreneurial talents of these three caused them to look at things in a new way. They saw new ways of doing church and experiencing God, and they led the group in that direction. This team of coequal leaders helped to establish the core DNA of the church and to carry the vision they believed God gave them, which was to build a covenant community of believers who would serve the purposes of God throughout the Ephrata area.

They called themselves "Servants of Love Community Church." Following the example of Jesus, they chose to make themselves servants of God and of one another. Although they recognized a variety of motives men have for serving, they believed that the purest of all was love. Love was the driving force behind the life and ministry of Jesus. They realized that "Servants of Love" was a hard name to live up to, but they trusted that by God's grace, the church could live up to its call.

A LOAF OF BREAD AND A CUP OF WINE

They chose a loaf of bread and a cup of wine for their logo. The loaf of bread was chosen as a symbol of Christ's body. Jesus said, "I am the Bread of Life." Today, after His death and resurrection, although He doesn't physically walk on earth anymore, His body is still manifested on earth through people. The cup of wine was chosen as a symbol of the blood of Christ, which was poured out as a sacrifice for the forgiveness of sins. It is through His blood that believers are redeemed, justified, and cleansed. They become overcomers and triumph over Satan by the blood of the

Initial logo for Servants of Love Community Church, 1977.

Lamb. It is His life-giving blood that continues to flow through His body of believers. The cup and the loaf together represent covenant. All through Old Testament and New Testament times, these symbols were used to seal a covenant.

The pursuit of God and experiencing His presence had become an exciting adventure for this small church. They learned to know Him and the power of the Holy Spirit, and it ignited a hunger in them for even more. They desired God not just for themselves, but they wanted other people to know the Lord in the same way. As God smiled on the condition of their hearts, He continued to lead them and gather this little flock under His wing.

LIVING ROOM TO LIVING ROOM

Initially, the church of twelve met in various homes. Barry and Cheryl Wissler were just married a couple of weeks when the church met for the first time. One of the first meetings was in the small living room of their mobile home on Clearview Road in Clay. At that time, the twelve never intended their gatherings to grow to the size of a traditional or

Community meal shared by members, ca. 1978.

First members' retreat, ca. 1978.

large church. Little did they know God's plan for them was more than they could ever think or imagine. They were just a handful of couples and a few singles who loved to worship the Lord together, felt called to support one another in their pursuit of God, and just enjoyed fellowship. Through the many changes and transitions that would come in the years to follow, the church continued to retain its relational emphasis and freedom in worship. These traits, evident at Ephrata Community Church today, were rooted in its very birth as a congregation.

Their pursuit of a community lifestyle led to involvement and commitment in the following ways:

- **Working Together**: They worked together on many projects, such as remodeling homes, working in gardens, etc.
- **Prayer**: This became an essential part of their Christian walk. They knew they had brothers and sisters standing with them in prayer no matter how tough the situation.
- **Worship**: They knew they were created to worship the Lord and spent a lot of time worshipping together.
- **Physical Conditioning**: They often played recreational activities like volleyball, baseball, and basketball to keep their bodies in good physical condition.
- **Relationships**: With an emphasis on relationships and connectedness, some of the singles moved in with married couples.
- **Intentional Community Living**: They purposed to live their lives openly before each other.

- **Evangelism**: Their greatest emphasis was always on people coming to know Jesus as their personal Savior and Lord.

LORDSHIP OF JESUS CHRIST

The primary vision and desire of the group was to bring the Lordship of Jesus Christ over their lives and the environment around them. To accomplish this, they chose to live their lives in a manner that would glorify and honor God and to speak God's Word in a liberating way. Judy (Martin) Groff stated, "The emphasis was that we didn't want to just have meetings together, but we wanted to live life together. I know that I would not be the person I am today had I not walked out my Christian life with this group. That's what we were about - walking out our Christian lives together."

The heart and passion of the small church formed a nucleus. It formed a DNA stamp. Everything that ECC is today, God, in His wisdom, put in place forty years ago when this group first formed. They had a holy passion to know God and to make Him known. They met God through Jesus Christ and the power of the Holy Spirit, and their desire was for others to meet Him in the same transforming way.

Aerial view of Wissler farm with renovated barn in the middle, ca. 1986.

A COMMUNITY CENTER

A CHICKEN BARN

In March 1978, Glenn and Mildred Wissler, (Barry's parents) graciously offered the church the use of an old barn that previously housed chickens. The barn was located on 70 Clay School Road in Clay Township. The group had a desire to reach youth in the neighboring mobile home park, which inspired them to transform the barn into a community youth center. With limited resources, they volunteered their time and gave many evenings and weekends to the project, beginning with the dirty and dusty work of dismantling and removing floors covered with chicken dirt. Many hours were spent adding a ceiling, insulation, wood paneling, lighting, and an addition for an office and bathrooms, while trying to use the cheapest materials available with their limited budget. With an understanding of working together in community, both men and women were committed to physically working on the project, which was affectionately referred to as "the shed" by the group. Accidents did happen, and mistakes were made, like the time Barry Wissler sawed his leg and needed an emergency trip to the hospital. Years later, the group enjoyed a good laugh when they realized that their pastor had literally shed his blood for the church!

Chicken barn before it was remodeled, 1978.

Interior floors of chicken barn being removed, 1978.

As the work progressed, there was a growing sense that God wanted to do something special on the property. During one particular discussion in the living room of Glenn and Mildred Wissler, vision was imparted to the members of the church, which became significant in the enlargement and encouragement of their dreams. Each member of the group, now numbering 18, shared the vision that God had given them of future ministry possibilities. These included counseling, evangelizing, teaching, book writing, worship leading, photography, women's ministry, youth ministry, pastoring, caring for the community, leading a discipleship school and Christian school and/or preschool program, owning a restaurant, building a community park, opening a retirement home, interceding for the community, praying for the sick, spiritual warfare initiatives, giving financial instruction, leading a children's choir, writing poetry, owning a business as ministry, operating a bookstore, and more. And from the vantage point of 40 years gone by, ECC has seen many of these visions and dreams become reality! God watered these early seeds, and in His timing, these dreams have become ministries inside and outside the church.

Church used the barn for the first time on New Year's Eve and played volleyball, December 31, 1978.

NEW YEAR'S EVE CELEBRATION

Even though the work on "the shed" was not complete, the church decided to celebrate their progress by cleaning it for a New Year's Eve Party on December 31, 1978. The plywood floors were mopped to remove the dust, and the room was cleared of building supplies and cleaned up. What a celebration that first event was! The group played volleyball and table games, and they celebrated months of hard work with a full spread of food. That winter, finishing touches were completed, including carpet laid in such a way that it could be rolled back to make room for a volleyball game.

A HOME FOR THE CHURCH

While their vision for a community youth center never materialized, the barn eventually became the home of the Servants of Love Community Church in the spring of 1979. The tiny congregation grew to about 24 members within the first year. After meeting in living rooms for over a year, the new space felt exceptionally large. Initially, they met in a circle at one end of the barn, wondering if they would ever fill it. As grateful

Membership totaled 24 with one child in March 1979.

Worship service in spring of 1979.

Community Center finished in spring of 1979.

as they were for a building, the group knew it was not the church. The church was the people, and so they purposed to refer to the building as "The Center."

With a larger meeting room, worship began to change with other instruments added to the several guitars. There was room for a piano, played by Judy (Martin) Groff, and drums played by Don Weber. These added a new dynamic to worship, but the goal of the team was always the same—to bring the presence of God into the meetings through their instruments, rather than simply excelling on their instruments.

The fledgling little church became known as "the bunch" that meets "up there in the barn." As they began to grow in faith and size, baptisms followed in the pond at Glenn and Mildred Wissler's farm. And with a congregation of mostly young adults, weddings were inevitable and frequently conducted in the building. Upon completion of the barn, this community-minded group turned their attention to helping each other. As the young couples bought homes for themselves, the group joined together in fixing up these houses. If help was needed to strip wallpaper, paint, or clean, it was assumed that the whole group would arrive for the project. As they served the Lord through serving each other, their relationships and commitments grew deep within the group.

INSTALLATION OF PASTOR BARRY WISSLER

LEADERSHIP CHANGE

The church grew slowly in its formative years, which allowed members to develop closer relationships. As this foundational strength grew deeper and stronger, it also became apparent that if they were to continue to move forward as a church, there would need to be necessary changes and adjustments along the way. The church had begun with a team of three pastors in a coequal leadership structure. There was good team-work, but the structure lacked a way to resolve differences and needed a clear vision carrier.

In early 1981, under the prompting of the Holy Spirit, John Weaver and Ray Martin approached Barry Wissler and asked if he would consider a lead elder role. After much prayer and discernment of God's will, Barry acknowledged the calling of God on his life and accepted the offer. The church as a whole recognized Barry's pastoral calling and was in full agreement with the decision. On April 1, 1981, Barry Wissler was formally installed as the first pastor of the church. The transition from co-equal leadership to a lead pastor went very well and became the first notable shift in the vision and structure of the church. This little congregation had passed the test and had bent their will in obedience to their Father. God was gently and graciously guiding them toward their destiny as they submitted to His leading.

A 37-YEAR JOURNEY BEGINS

Barry Wissler began the journey of leading the church for the next 37 years. He commenced building the church on the strength of relationships within a community that was grounded in the Word and embracing the life of the Holy Spirit. Barry had a real gift of practical preaching that was easy for people to follow and apply to their lives. As a pastor, he modeled the accessibility and friendship of leadership. Not

Pastor Barry Wissler preached many messages in the barn, ca. 1984.

only was he a pastor, but he was also a friend to the members of the church. He led the congregation by example in how to love and care for one another even during difficult times.

In these formative years, the church became rather preoccupied with themselves, looking mostly inward at their own lives and relationships. They lacked connections with other believers and received a lot of their teaching through cassette tapes and magazines. These mostly came from the "Shepherding Movement" that originated out of Ft. Lauderdale, Florida under the ministry of Bob Mumford, Charles Simpson, Derek Prince, Don Basham, and Ern Baxter. This movement arose out of a concern and need for effective discipleship in the body of Christ. The teaching from this movement struck a common chord with this small group of believers, who wanted to grow as disciples of Christ and walk together in that discipleship. Encountering God and walking it out through intentional relationships was a new concept for them. It became a foundational teaching and a key part of the group's identity as they continued to grow.

While the Shepherding Movement tended to overcorrect some of the need for discipleship by encouraging believers to submit unconditionally to more mature Christians, the church never fully embraced this teaching. To bring balance, Barry Wissler introduced the biblical teaching of the priesthood of all believers, which taught that all believers have direct access to God through prayer without requiring a human mediator. While good counsel is beneficial, each person can know God for himself. Barry taught the importance of everyone having a personal relationship with the true and living God, while recognizing that believers also need one another and are family in the body of Christ. Both the vertical relationship with God and the horizontal relationship with each other were needed and vital to the thriving, growing church. This foundational teaching of connecting both to God and to others has carried through to ECC today and remains its core desire. Even then, God was faithfully nurturing and guiding this infant church into its greater destiny.

RAY CIERVO

During these early years, Barry Wissler, with the wisdom of God, understood the dangers of walking alone as a pastor without spiritual oversight. His one condition before accepting the position of pastor was that he could find a mentor. He felt he needed someone who could advise him in his spiritual life, as well as in pastoring a church. During his first summer as pastor, he attended a weeklong Bible school entitled "Jesus Feast"

Ray Ciervo.

at Landisville Campgrounds in Landisville, Pennsylvania. This God-ordained encounter would change Barry's life and the future of the church. Through Malcolm Smith's teaching on "Knowing God" and Ray Ciervo's instruction on the book of Romans, Barry experienced vivid dreams that significantly expanded and deepened his view of God.

Ray Ciervo was a pastor from New Jersey who oversaw a network of churches. The timing was right for Barry to define his relationship with Ray Ciervo as his pastor and mentor. This relationship also linked the church to a group of churches on the East Coast and England through Ray's network, Edification Ministries. This network relationship was formalized on October 2, 1981. Three years after becoming the pastor, Ray Ciervo officially ordained Barry in the role, commissioning him by the laying on of hands, on December 21, 1984.

HOUSEHOLD GROUPS

EPHRATA AND CLAY

With a pastor in place and the church growing, the need to connect in smaller groups became evident. In April 1982, the church established it's first "household groups" in Ephrata and Clay. These household groups were small groups of approximately five to ten people, who met geographically on a weekly basis to provide pastoral care and fellowship for members. During these times of fellowship, many things took place, including the sharing of personal needs, praying for one another, encouraging one another, reproving and correcting one another, etc. The household meetings varied from a more organized format of teaching and sharing to more informal times of playing tennis, visiting with elderly people, or eating out together. The household leaders planned the activities to help the individual members of the group learn to know one another better, which resulted in strong, connected relationships.

During an interview with some of the earliest members of the church, Dale Martin recalled, "The fellowship is one of my favorite stories of our church—one that has occurred many times over the years. I enjoyed sitting around in someone's home and having good wholesome fellowship. I would go home thinking, 'I am full'... feeling full and rich. And it is based on the deep, meaningful relationships we have together with the Lord and with each other. Good friends who appreciate and value the same things I do and who are real. You connect not only emotionally, but spiritually as well."

Initially, the purpose of smaller group meetings was for pastoral care, but during the mid 1980s, as God was gently turning the group outward, the leadership realized that they could also be used for outreach. The vision of multiplying groups began to change the view and purpose of small groups. This was a difficult transition because the home groups were originally birthed for relationships within the church body. The outward focus to the unchurched was a stretch for this group of believers. God was faithfully directing and preparing the congregation for a major shift.

LOOKING BEYOND THEMSELVES 1982 – 1993

RAY CIERVO AND EDIFICATION MINISTRIES

The mentoring relationship between Barry Wissler and Ray Ciervo proved to be a divine connection. Ray taught the young, inexperienced pastor in his early twenties how to care for the flock and build the foundations of the group into a functioning church. Through Ray's teaching and guidance, Barry was introduced to Reformed Theology, which became instrumental in guiding him to study at Westminster Seminary in later years.

INTRODUCING THE KINGDOM OF GOD

Not only was the mentoring relationship good for Barry, it was also good for the small, and mostly isolated, young church. Ray Ciervo introduced the foundational teaching of the Kingdom of God. He defined God's Kingdom as the place "where God works out His purposes against His enemies." As believers join God in this process of advancing His Kingdom, the culture around them is transformed. The church was encouraged to develop a relationship with God instead of settling for only a concept of Him. In addition to an individual response to His Kingdom, a corporate response was also required. Ray was committed to building churches by making disciples to spread the Gospel and impact

Servants of Love Community Church, 1984.

the world with the power of the Kingdom. This required living in the righteousness of the Kingdom and persevering through trials.

Through Ray's continuous teaching, the church realized the importance of their foundation, vision, and strategy. These all played a part in the life of the church and helped to shape its identity. But there was more. Ray taught that the church can grow and strengthen when relationships are built among believers under the headship of Jesus Christ. The scriptural foundations, biblical vision, and strategy would unite them in a common purpose to build together. But if they were going to grow and fulfill their God-given calling, they must have a corporate vision. That vision would establish their goals and policies for the church. The church would become a sort of caravan, moving forward together to spread the Gospel to the world, not existing solely for its own needs and happiness. The vision of the church began to take a significant turn at this time. While the formative years were focused inward, the church embraced this new direction and turned outward with a renewed interest in evangelism and outreach.

Worship service, 1984.

Ray Ciervo's network of churches, Edification Ministries (which later became New Covenant Ministries), had many facets and spanned several continents. His influential role with other pastors and leaders connected the church with the larger body of Christ nationally and internationally, as many speakers and groups came and spent time among its members. A major aspect of the network included the strengthening of churches through teaching and preaching at seminars, conferences, and Bible schools.

SUMMER FAMILY CONFERENCE

The church was introduced to Edification Ministries Summer Family Conferences in the summer of 1982 which was held on a university campus in Trenton, New Jersey. Over the next 13 years, the annual weeklong conference became a major event in the life of the congregation as God saved people, and lives were changed. It was a time set apart for entire families. Each year, they loaded cribs, strollers, big wheels, and bikes onto their cars and minivans and headed for a university campus or retreat center in New Jersey, New York, Virginia, or Pennsylvania. All meals were provided, as was care for the youngest children, called "night patrol," during the evening meetings. Classes for children, recreation, and seminars were available during the day.

Throughout the retreat week, believers from many congregations in the network came together as one body to set apart a time to meet with the Lord and allow Him to speak and minister to them individually and corporately. Each year was a bit different in direction, yet the vision God imparted became sharper and clearer. It was a great privilege for the church to be part of a company of committed people, united in a vision of the kingdom of God, and called to serve Him in His purposes on the earth. The yearly summer conferences became a special and unique time for the church as they anticipated times of refreshment, teaching, worship, and rich fellowship among the other churches. Many lasting friendships were forged during these weeklong events. The atmosphere was saturated with expectancy, as up to 900 gathered to worship together and hear the Word of the Lord preached from gifted ministers.

FIRST SHORT-TERM MISSION TRIP

As God continued to steer the church to look beyond themselves, they soon recognized the emphasis God placed on spreading the gospel to the whole world. Within two years of the relationship forming with Ray Ciervo and Edification Ministries, God provided an opportunity to link the church to foreign missions in a tangible way.

GUYANA, SOUTH AMERICA
Through Ray Ciervo's connections, word came that a construction team was needed to build an orphanage in Guyana, South America. Excitement rose in the church as they discovered that Guyana was located on the northern shore of South America and was originally a British colony. Therefore, the language spoken was English and would not present communication problems for the team. Answering the call to go were Ray Martin, Glenn Weaver, and Mark Ulrich, along with several others from Ray Ciervo's network of churches. In October 1983, the church sent the

three men on what would become ECC's first short-term missions trip.

They were headed to a small Christian cooperative village, Haura-runi, which was carved out of the dense tropical jungle in the interior of Guyana and away from the security of civilization. Seven years earlier, 70 Guyanese Christians had cleared and settled on a plot of land they had received from the government. Their vision was to build a community as a base to preach the gospel, which would have prophetic significance to the region and nation. This village needed an orphanage to house the orphans in their midst.

Upon arrival in Guyana, the team received a hostile reception from the government. Their hosts from the village navigated them through customs and visa issues, and they finally made their way to Hauraruni, where they found themselves in very primitive and undeveloped con-ditions. There was no phone connection, and the only communication that the church received for the duration of the two-week trip was that they had safely arrived at the Georgetown airport. After working in the hot and sticky rainforest climate, bathing in the creek was preferred to washing out of a bucket. Despite the conditions, the team found themselves falling in love with the Guyanese people groups who were comprised of Africans, East Indians, and Amerindians.

Villagers joined the missions team to complete the orphanage, 1983.

This first mission trip allowed the congregation to begin to grasp the heart of God for the uttermost parts of the world. The country of Guyana found a special place in the heart of the church. The following year, they sent Barry Wissler to accompany Ray Ciervo to teach at the Bible School. God had opened the door to international missions.

The Guyanese village grew as a base for camps, conferences, leadership seminars, and training schools under the leadership of Philip Mohabir of Guyana. Financial support for orphans and churches was sent, along with shipments of supplies. As government regulations relaxed and it became easier and safer, more construction teams were sent throughout the years to build classrooms, dormitories, a missionary house, and a chapel. Barry made numerous trips to minister in the Bible School.

Through the years, the work expanded to other churches and towns in Guyana to meet needs in construction, preaching, teaching, and conducting children's events. After 34 years, the church's involvement in Guyana continues and has extended to working with Pastor Ovid Schultz of Balm of Gilead Church in Berbice and the YWAM base in Parika under the directorship of Kim Cook.

Little did the congregation know that a first-time trip to an unknown little country in South America would set in motion a domino chain of events that would literally lead to worldwide missions. Through contacts in Guyana and obedience to the Holy Spirit, Barry traveled to England next, thus leading the church to answer the call of God's heart to reach the nations.

SPREADING THE GOSPEL

As the heart of the congregation turned outward, they began to take seriously God's will and call to spread the gospel. The church members desired to fulfill their call as disciples of Christ and to share the gospel

Shoofly pie and ice cream sold at the Ephrata Street Fair as the first outreach to the community, September 1984.

in effective ways within the Ephrata community. The leadership team began to equip the church for the work of evangelism, and this thrust drove the church to pray for boldness as they pursued the true meaning of making disciples. They understood Christ's model of discipleship to mean mature believers training and teaching less mature believers and together moving the church forward to accomplish the will of God.

As the town of Ephrata was preparing for their annual street fair in September 1984, the church felt it would be a great opportunity to introduce themselves to the community at this event. So they built a small trailer, obtained a spot on the street, baked many shoofly pies, and sold slices with ice cream. This event was the first of many the church did to intentionally reach the community.

NEW NAME—EPHRATA COMMUNITY CHURCH

By the mid 1980s, as the church was transitioning from an ingrown community of believers to reaching out to the local community, they

First logo of Ephrata Community Church, April 17, 1985.

realized another name was necessary. After prayer and discernment, they chose Ephrata Community Church. The words "Community Church" described them well because they were a church of people that were built together into a community of believers. This name also spoke a message about their interest to be involved with the people of Ephrata and the fact that they were taking on the identity of this particular locality. The name was general enough to keep them from being identified with a particular movement or emphasis of teaching, which they felt would prove to be helpful in evangelism. Along with a new name, they updated their logo including the cross, bread, and wine. The new name and logo were officially adopted on April 17, 1985. A few years later the tagline, "Join our growing vision" was added.

TOUCHING THE COMMUNITY

In 1985, the church began a project to survey the people living within the Ephrata Borough so that they could better understand the community. They went in groups of two, door to door, asking a set of twelve questions. The questions ranged from involvement in church, concerns in the area, to their contact with newspaper, radio, and TV. The purpose of the survey was to discover ways in which Ephrata Community Church could serve the residents of the community. When appropriate, they left literature about the church. They worked on this survey through the summer and picked it up again the following spring.

With the focus now being outward, the church found increasingly creative ways to reach the community. Small events such as a Lititz home group hosting a video seminar called "What the Bible Says About Child Training" to large events such as a church-sponsored community yard sale were organized to be able to get to know neighbors.

The need for training in evangelism became apparent as they began to reach out to the community. Through Glad Tidings School of Evangelism and Mark McGrath's Evangelism Training Program, God planted his vision for evangelism within their hearts. Realizing that the effort of evangelism by the members placed the church in a position for attack from the enemy and in need of strategizing, a prayer emphasis was started. Prayer meetings began to take center stage, and several were held throughout the week.

CLAY AFTER SCHOOL PROGRAM

On January 4, 1988, the Clay After School Program opened as a way to reach the community and became one that would glorify God in every way. This program, directed by Daphne Keim, marked a time of new beginnings for the church. The program was designed as a service for working parents. It provided a way for children to be supervised during the time between school dismissal and parents' arrival from work. Children were brought to the church building on the school bus and enjoyed snacks, group activities, and homework assistance.

Clay After School Program served the local Clay Elementary School, ca. 1988.

CELEBRATING 40 YEARS OF GOD'S FAITHFULNESS

OUTREACH INTO THE COMMUNITY

By 1988, the growth of the church began to accelerate as it became more evangelistic. The church added home groups in Reamstown, Reinholds, Brickerville, and Lititz. By this time, the church began to entertain the idea that they might outgrow the barn and would soon need another building. So on April 17, 1988, the first building fund offering was taken.

The outreach into the community continued in September 1989, as the church sent over 16,000 ECC church brochures to residents in Akron, Denver, Ephrata, Lititz, and Stevens through the local Shopping News.

In another effort to reach the children of the area, the men of the congregation began the Christian Service Brigade to reach boys ages 8–12. Beginning on September 11, 1990, they met weekly for games, projects, and stories. The boys were divided into small groups called posts, and each post was led by a Christian male leader called a ranger. The boys learned about God's Word and were introduced to Jesus Christ and the life of discipleship and service that Christ called them to live.

Clay area home group at Glenn and Kay Weaver's home, ca. 1986.

Within a year a Pioneer Girls Club with a similar format was started for girls. The leaders of both programs were passionate about reaching the children in the church and community for Christ.

FROM FARM BOY TO SEMINARY GRADUATE

The journey from a farm boy farming with his father to a full-time pastor was not an easy one for Barry Wissler. Initially coleading with two others, Barry was given one day a week off from farming responsibilities to study and prepare his message. At twenty-three years old, married to Cheryl, and expecting their first child, Barry was installed as pastor of the little group of believers. During the first few years, Barry juggled his responsibilities between farming, pastoring, and raising his young family. The church compensated him for one day a week. A son, David, and daughter, Jessica, were added to his family in these early years.

After pastoring for five years and with a motivation to improve his writing skills, Barry decided to take a writing class at F&M College.

Barry, Cheryl, David, and Jessica Wissler, 1984.

A love for education and learning soon led to more classes at Millersville University. During these years, God deposited a hunger within him to understand the Bible in a deeper way. Barry's mentor, Ray Ciervo, suggested that he enroll in a program at the Center of Urban Theological Studies (CUTS) in Philadelphia, which was affiliated with Geneva College. So in addition to farming, pastoring, and caring for his young family, Barry began to commute to Philadelphia several times a week for class.

Attending CUTS in the city of Philadelphia was a stretch for the onetime farm boy raised in a rural Republican family. Most of the students were African American and Democrats. The studies changed his worldview as he began to realize that the Bible was for all spheres of life, including business and politics. As he read and studied the writings of the Dutch reformers, he was exposed to reformed theology and gained a deeper understanding of the Kingdom of God. Over this period of time, Barry's salary was gradually increased to three days a week. After many semesters with a heavy load of classwork, Barry graduated from Geneva College in May 1989 with a B.A. in Biblical Studies.

The church began to grow significantly in the late 80s and early 90s, at which time ECC was finally able to support a full-time pastor. After more than ten years as a part-time pastor, Barry became Ephrata Community Church's full-time pastor in early 1992. With a desire to learn more in order to lead the church most effectively, he enrolled in Westminster Theology Seminary in Philadelphia. Some of his professors from CUTS were also professors at Westminster, making it a natural fit to resume his studies there. In June 1996, Barry graduated with a master's degree in Religion.

The journey from farm boy to seminary graduate took almost 20 years and was a time of many sacrifices for Barry, Cheryl, and their family. At the same time, Barry felt the support of his family and church community as he pursued his pastoral training. God was setting the wheels in motion for the calling on Barry's life and the destiny of ECC.

TEN YEARS OLD

"Another chapter of our church history is about to begin. After being together now for ten years, God has been establishing and preparing us. We now understand that we exist not for ourselves but for His purposes and for others.

I believe that God is giving us another beginning—a fresh start! God said in Isaiah, 'Behold I will do something new, now it will spring forth.' Our God is a God of new things, continually leading us on by His Spirit. Often 'old things pass away and new things come.'" (Isaiah 43:19 NASB) – *Barry Wissler*

The first ten years of life for Ephrata Community Church were a testimony to the faithfulness of God. He had protected and led the church through various stages and changes. He had delivered them from several pitfalls and established them with a clear sense of purpose and vision. They believed God had prepared them for a future of fruitful service to Him. And so, with expectancy, they prayed that they would discover and embrace the future that He destined for them.

The 10-year celebration weekend was held on October 16-18, 1987. Friday night was geared for families with a "Shindig in the Barn," which

Ephrata Community Church, 1987.

"Shindig in the Barn" was a highlight of the 10-year anniversary, October 1987.

was held in the big old farm barn on the property. The night included a hayride, food, and skits. Celebration meetings were held on Saturday night and Sunday morning with guest speaker Ray Ciervo. The weekend concluded with a banquet dinner at the Treadway Resort Inn in Lancaster with Ray Ciervo, a choral group, and worship. Pastors from Ray's network also attended and joined in the celebration.

The words that Ray Ciervo spoke over Ephrata Community Church that weekend proved to be prophetic. "We must have an identity of being a sent people. God has commissioned us to this earth. We must see ourselves as being sent to the ends. He sent us to be apostolic, prophetic, and evangelistic. Winning people to the Lord, standing against injustices, and proclaiming righteousness, or whether we are out seeking to plant churches and establish local communities on this planet, we are life and salt to this earth…

…In and of ourselves when we look at the insurmountable tasks that are in front of us, we don't have a whole lot of anything. The thing that makes us different is that Jesus is among us. It's what makes us the people that are sent. When Jesus sends, He'll go with us. Take your commission seriously that you are a sent people. You are not a passive people who are just planted, like a brick in the ground. You are supposed to multiply and grow and expand in all kinds of supernatural things. There isn't a method to make it work. What makes us different is that

Jesus is here. What makes you special is that Jesus is here. No more, no less, just Jesus. It doesn't depend on us. Our real resource is Him. The real gifting is Him. See Him in each other.

I want to encourage you today that the way to be sent is to be a blessing to this world. The way you are a blessing to this world is by letting Christ live in you. Let Jesus stand in your midst; let Him live in your midst. It's not because of anything special in us, except Christ. It's because Jesus has been here. And what is going to get you through the next 10 or 20 or 30, is not learning how to do it, it is recognizing His place, recognizing what He wants from you. I think God has some fruitful years for you. God can use everything you did right and everything you did wrong, because He is here. Jesus said, 'As I have been sent, so send I you.'" (message condensed)

As the congregation looked back that weekend, they could see that God had poured out His Holy Spirit into the group of young believers and had faithfully brought them on a 10-year journey. No matter what was ahead, they were ready to face it, because they knew that God had more for them. He wasn't done with them yet. And so it was fitting that they ended the weekend by joining together in singing the song "He Brought Us Out."

He Brought Us Out
by Renzo Fidani

He did not bring us out this far
To take us back again
He brought us out to take us in
To the promised land

Tho' there be giants in the land
We will not be afraid
He brought us out to take us in
To the promised land

45

PRESSING ON—MISSION AND VISION

With ten years behind them as a church and a real sense of purpose, Ephrata Community Church continued to grow and increase. With that increase, the Lord raised up another man to serve in an elder role to help oversee and care for the church. The church acknowledged and recognized God's hand and the Holy Spirit's anointing on Mark Ulrich. Ray Ciervo ordained him as an elder in December 1987, with a group of network pastors and ECC elders laying hands on and commissioning him for the work of ministry. The ordination of Mark, with the support of his wife, Marlene, was yet another example for the congregation of God's provision and faithfulness in providing leadership and care for them.

With a renewed sense of purpose and leadership in place, the church prepared to further define their vision and mission—to establish a clearer focus on what God was calling them to do. They understood that they were to glorify God foremost, but they needed to flesh out the "how" of walking this out. After much prayer and discussion, the Holy Spirit revealed this mission:

Elder ordination of Mark Ulrich, December 12, 1987. His wife, Marlene, is on the right.

The Mission of ECC is to glorify God by
Proclaiming the gospel
Preparing workers
Producing disciples
Planting churches

He further broke it down as follows:

Proclaiming the Gospel
Worldwide evangelism
Beginning with our own neighborhoods
Going into all the world
Producing Disciples
Teaching believers to obey Christ
Training through relationships
Discover life purpose and your spiritual gifts
Planting Churches
Church planting is most effective form of evangelism
The ancient church of Antioch is our model
Preparing Workers
"Lord send workers into the harvest"
Effective workers need training
Our training center will help prepare workers

SIGNIFICANT RETREAT—1990

As Barry Wissler sat in a service in Bartica, a church in the interior rain forest of Guyana, God began to sow a seed in his heart. Bartica was a little church of 120 indigenous people. They were already reaching five Amerindian villages in the interior where they had to walk by foot or travel upstream by boat. This small church had a vision of several more villages that they wanted to reach. They had sent several men and women to Bible school who were now pastoring in other areas. Barry saw a little church, not impressive, but making an impact on the country of

Guyana. In that moment, the Lord revealed to his heart that the church at Ephrata could be like this little church, a model of an Antioch church. As he returned to Hauruni, he began thinking about their training center and how it was preparing people for missions. He was convinced that having a call and fervency for the work of God is one thing, but being trained skillfully is quite another thing. He saw not only a church that was focused on the world and mission-oriented, but also a church that effectively trained its people and sent them out into the mission field. As Barry pondered this new revelation and direction for the church, God also began to prepare the hearts of the church members.

ANTIOCH CHURCH MODEL

In April 1990, the church leadership decided to take the church on a weekend retreat to Black Rock Retreat Center. It was designed to be a time of fellowship, teaching, and hearing God for the church. Barry sensed by the Holy Spirit that the timing was right to share with ECC about the Antioch model of church life found in the New Testament. The church at Antioch had made the first and one of the most profound impacts on the rest of the world. From Antioch, believers had spread the gospel to the whole Roman Empire and became a mother church for many of the churches in Asia Minor. Reaching the Gentile world became the mission of the Antioch church. They focused on the world and were not afraid of it or of its sinful ways. They did not seclude and isolate themselves from the world, but rather went out boldly into it. The Antioch church crossed religious, racial, and cultural boundaries. They shared the gospel with boldness to a people who were different from themselves.

Barry Wissler shares the Antioch church model at the retreat in April 1990.

The Antioch church grew and sent out Paul and Barnabas, supporting them generously as missionaries of the early church. The apostolic churches planted by Paul were connected to Antioch, the sending church. Since Antioch was the center for theological studies and training, they prepared, sent, and supported workers to plant churches in other areas. The Gentile world was reached by a movement that started in Antioch, first initiated by the Holy Spirit.

Antioch was striking at the mission of God for His people: A church not existing for itself. Barry challenged Ephrata Community Church to become an Antioch church. He encouraged the church, saying "I want you to be committed to our local church. Even more so, I want you to be committed to God and His larger purposes on the earth."

Taking on the Antioch model for ECC would need to be an act of faith as they expanded the work God had for them. Specifically, it would require more of the church's finances. While ECC was already a generous church and gave away 30-40% of its funds, this endeavor would require more. With an eye to God's larger purposes on the earth, they could not be as protective of their own assets and care for themselves. Barry continually affirmed that this focus would keep them from drifting out of God's purposes and stagnating as a church. However, it was crucial that they begin to find ways to take the gospel to the unbelieving and unchurched in their area.

That day, Ephrata Community Church agreed to adopt Antioch as their church model moving forward. But that was not God's only word for them that weekend.

PROPHETIC WORD—"IN THE FOURTH YEAR"

Later that day at the retreat, God spoke very clearly through a prophetic word, stating that, "in the fourth year, I will pour out my Spirit." The church had just chosen to model itself after the early church of Antioch and, therefore, interpreted the word as a call to prepare for harvest in four years. The elders of ECC, agreeing that this was an accurate word from God, concluded that by 1994 they would have a core group of people ready to plant a church. They felt they needed to create "new wineskins" to hold the new wine. Of course, they had no idea or context for what the outpouring of the Holy Spirit might look like. Through Barry's study of the Antioch church, missions and church planting were the most effective means toward world evangelization. The church focused on Acts 1:8, promising that: "You shall receive power when the Holy Spirit has come upon you; and you shall be My witnesses both in Jerusalem, and in all Judea and Samaria, and even to the remotest part of the earth." (NASB)

The church left the retreat having adopted the mission of world evangelism through apostolic-like ministry. With the prophetic word in their hearts, they were willing to give themselves to the body of Christ wherever that may be. They would pursue the training and development of leaders, sending them out locally and internationally. They desired to become cross-cultural in their work, while operating in the five-fold ministry gifts. They wanted to be a receiving and a sending church. They wanted to plant churches. They didn't know how all of these desires and the prophetic word that they had received would come into fruition, but they had faith and were willing to act upon it in preparation for the next four years.

Over the course of Ephrata Community Church's history, there were several key moments when God intervened and defined them as a body of believers. The weekend retreat in 1990 was one such event. Not only did ECC embrace the Antioch church model, but there was also a prophetic word that would lie dormant for four years without any clear understanding about what was to come through it. Was there more to the prophecy than simply planting a church?

THE PROPHETIC GIFT IS INTRODUCED

As Barry continued to study the church at Antioch, he received the revelation that it was the gift of prophecy and prophetic words within the church that provided the power for the church to move forward. At the same weekend retreat, along with teaching on the Antioch church, Barry taught a message on "The Place of Prophecy in the Church." He shared that the prophets are the ones who build up, stir up, and cheer up. Without prophecy, the church misses something. It is the prophetic that provides the fire to keep things going. Barry taught that a prophet is one who presents a word from God to men and that all should desire earnestly to prophesy, as is encouraged in 1 Corinthians. Authentic prophecy will edify, exhort, and console. While all are able to prophesy, some are gifted and excel in this area of ministry.

LEON PRICE

Two months later, to introduce the church to prophecy in a more tangible way, the leadership invited a prophet for a weekend of meetings. Following a day of prayer and fasting by the church, Leon Price came to Ephrata Community Church for the first time in June 1990. Leon was a seasoned prophet and a true "eyewitness to history," having seen and participated in numerous movements of the Lord across the nation. He had a unique blend of spiritual sensitivity, personal maturity, and theological integrity that enabled him to move through a wide range of sovereign visitations.

God, in His faithfulness, had brought an authentic prophet to introduce the church to the prophetic gift. After Leon preached the first night, he began to minister to individual members. The whole church could hear the individual prophecies, and amazement spread among them about the accuracy of his words. Without foreknowledge of any of the peoples' lives or situations, he would speak directly and accurately, encouraging them in their giftings and callings and bringing a life-changing moment to many. Leon's prophetic words built up both the individual members, as well the corporate church body. His love for the church

Leon Price.

51

was evident. He would minister for hours after a meeting, always concerned that everyone received a prophetic word.

Leon Price knew the importance of training the next generation. He eventually began to train others in the congregation to prophesy. He would work with them as a team and at times, with a twinkle in his eye, give them the microphone and say, "You do this one." With Leon by their side, they gained confidence in learning how to prophesy.

Leon Price believed his personal mission was to "Preach Righteousness, Show Love, Promote Unity, and Equip the Church." He returned on a yearly basis, each time imparting these values into the young church through his prophetic voice, biblical teaching, and a genuine love. This gentle, gracious, godly father figure became one of the most influential persons in the life of Ephrata Community Church. After ministering yearly at ECC for 19 years, he passed on to his eternal reward in 2009 at the age of 85. Through Leon Price, God further guided and loved the church into their identity.

CHURCH PLANTING FOCUS

In 1992, with a full-time pastor in place, it was very satisfying for the church to celebrate 15 years as a testimony to the faithfulness of God. Although the church was formed by a small group of young believers, God had faithfully watered what He had planted. He produced both numerical growth and spiritual maturity in the group. Within one year, the average attendance had climbed from 120 to 150 people, a 25 percent increase. More visitors were coming and staying. God's desire was to build a church whose people were knitted together in fellowship. Barry Wissler encouraged them to make these new relationships a priority, for a church built together, corporately, would be better able to receive the harvest of God and glorify Him.

On the 15th anniversary of the church, Barry wrote, "Our current

Ephrata Community Church, 1992.

challenge is to continue to follow God into His future for us, while remaining faithful to all that He has historically built into our foundations. The principles, which we have taught and sought to apply, should provide a base of strength for future growth. We want to continue to reach out into our communities with the gospel and incorporate all those that God brings to us for care. I look forward to the day when Ephrata Community Church can plant other congregations in Pennsylvania and send out some of our families as foreign missionaries. May God help us to be diligent workers in His harvest."

With the adoption of the Antioch church model and the prophetic word of harvest still in their hearts, a shift began to take place. Church planting became the new focus, along with the training and equipping of workers for the harvest.

NEW COVENANT MINISTRIES

Leading up to the 15-year celebration and contributing to the focus on equipping and sending out workers was the partnership of ECC and New Covenant Ministries (NCM). In 1990, Ray Ciervo of New Covenant Ministries (previously Edification Ministries) felt God leading him to move his office and ministry to Ephrata. The leadership saw this as an opportune time to work more closely with Ray, and they considered

Office building before and after renovations, 1990.

sharing office space. With the limited space in the barn, a concrete block shop on the farm was offered to the church as office space. The members once again put their hands to the work of transforming a farm workshop into offices.

With this new partnership came the opportunity to join with NCM in offering a video satellite school through Liberty Ministry Training Institute. The program was designed to aid local churches in preparing their members as teachers, group leaders, children's workers, elders, etc. It was intended for those who had little or no biblical or theological training, and so it became something that also benefitted the leaders of Ephrata Community Church.

As the church continued to grow, once again under the guidance of the Holy Spirit and confirmation of the church members, Ray Ciervo and the ECC elders laid hands on Ken Keim, with his wife, Daphne, by his side, and installed him as an elder in March 1993.

3

OUTPOURING OF THE HOLY SPIRIT 1994 – 1999

FIRST CHURCH PLANT

Following the prophetic word given at the retreat in 1990, church plant-ing became an important part of the church's vision. The timing seemed right, as Ephrata Community Church had been growing steadily. And it was obvious that unless steps were taken, the congregation would soon outgrow their facilities. After much prayer, the consensus was to plant a church rather than build a new building or add another service. God's vision for the first ECC church plant began to unfold.

In early 1993, a call was put forth to the church for members to begin seeking God individually about whether they should participate directly in the work of planting this second congregation. During this time, it became increasingly clear that Ken Keim, the newest elder, was being called by God to pastor this new church.

COVENANT COMMUNITY CHURCH

There were initially eleven families, totaling approximately 35 people, that responded to the call. They began meeting early on Sunday mornings before the corporate meeting to prepare for the church launch. After spending a significant time in prayer and strategizing, the group and the elders of ECC felt that God was directing the congregation towards the Centerville area, about 15 miles from ECC. The new congregation, Covenant Community Church, held their first meeting on Sunday, May 1, 1994. Barry Wissler continued to provide guidance to the church plant's founding pastor, Ken Keim, and ECC provided other resources to strengthen the church plant.

Ephrata Community Church elders and members operated with the revelation that if God was going to pour out His Spirit, new wineskins were needed. A new wineskin was now in place. With the new church plant, ECC had been obedient to the prophetic word from the retreat. But in the midst and excitement of launching Covenant Community Church, they had forgotten the part of the word about God pouring out His Spirit. They were so focused on the church plant and were not expecting what was about to happen next.

AND THEN IT HAPPENED...SUDDENLY

In Barry Wissler's own words, "The church had always believed in the gifts of the Spirit because our roots went back to the Jesus People and the Charismatic Movement. There would have been some gifts of the Spirit operating at different times in our meetings, but it wasn't prominent. Our worship was more charismatic and free. I turned to conservative evangelical theology for a number of years while I was going to seminary, being a little bit disheartened by what I saw in the Charismatic Movement. In 1994, I was in the middle of a Hebrew class in seminary.

I had heard about what was happening at a church in Toronto, Canada. I didn't want to have anything to do with it. Ray Ciervo, my mentor, had encouraged me to go, but I just wasn't interested, and I wouldn't go. Later, I was at a conference where they prayed for pastors, and a pastor from England—a friend of mine—prayed for me, and I received something. I was determined that I wasn't going to fall down when he prayed for me, but I did anyway. That night I began to dream.

And every night for four to six nights I would just dream constantly through the night. I would get awake, fall asleep, and have another dream. And so I knew something was building to the point where I believed God wanted to do another great awakening. I had been reading about the Great Awakening and the teachings of Jonathan Edwards for class.

After a week of dreaming I came to church on Sunday and preached a seven-point message on something about revival. It was a pretty uneventful sermon until point five which was on repentance. I noticed people began to cry, and I had a period during my preaching where something came over me and people started to weep. Then it lifted and I went on to give an altar call, which I rarely did. That day there were maybe 30–40 people who rushed front. Many were weeping and repenting and as I came down off the platform to pray for people, they started to fall over. That had never happened before. We didn't have anyone to catch them as they fell, and so they just crashed to the floor. It was sort of a wild meeting. But it was good. I knew it was God. There were good things started that day that continued on for some time."

A SOVEREIGN MOVE OF GOD

Taking the whole congregation off guard, this was the beginning of what became known as "The Renewal" at Ephrata Community Church. This season of renewal brought with it works of the Holy Spirit that were new to the church. While the church had heard about revivals like the Great Awakening, experiencing it was quite different. No matter what words are used to describe the renewal, they always fall short, because it was almost indescribable. It was simply a sovereign move of God and a time of tangibly experiencing His great goodness towards the church. People would come with their baggage and all the stuff that was wrong in their lives, and God would simply show up and meet them in a way that transformed lives instantly. What might normally take place over the course of six months, a year, five years, or even ten years, He was literally doing in seconds in people's lives.

At the time of this outpouring of God's Spirit, the small groups were meeting together for corporate prayer on Wednesday nights. Since the church was already together these evenings, they also became a time of prayer and ministry in addition to Sunday mornings. Ministry teams were trained how to pray for and minister to individuals, and "catchers" were trained how to break the fall of someone who became too weak to stand when the power of the Holy Spirit touched them.

The renewal meetings would begin with a time of worship lasting at least 45 minutes. A short exhortation was followed by an extended time of worship, during which a ministry team would pray for individuals. The worship team often led for hours during the ministry time, sometimes until two o'clock on a Sunday afternoon and midnight or later on Friday nights. But no one minded. People came and went as needed throughout the night, but many stayed the entire time not wanting to miss anything that God was doing. They simply enjoyed lingering in the presence of God, which felt refreshing, renewing, and intoxicating.

WORSHIP

Worship became a prominent focus during this time. It was often during corporate worship that God would touch people. They came with a hunger for God and with an expectancy to receive from Him. Worship leader Mark Ulrich stated, "With the first strum of the guitar, you were in the presence of God. People knew that's what they were there for. It was exciting to see people being touched during worship, weeping, with hands raised. The presence of God was everywhere, and you knew it was Him. I knew it was His anointing on the worship and not my skills in leading. He was so much bigger than we were."

Each time the church met, God continued to impart His Spirit to people. All kinds of powerful demonstrations happened during these meetings. People were delivered from demonic activity. Many were physically healed, and many others received fresh revelation from God. People weary from the frustrations of life received refreshment and found a release of new joy. Many fell in love with God all over again. God was

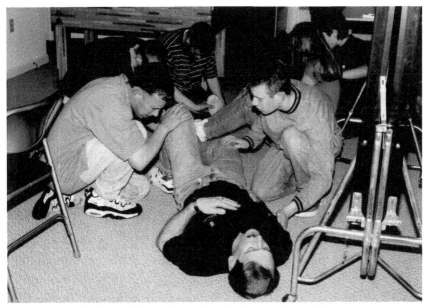
Passionate youth prayed for many during the Renewal, ca. 1996.

healing past hurts and was restoring relationships. People found freedom from bondages as they felt God's tangible presence and love. Prodigals came home and found a loving Father waiting for them. One young man, in particular, came bound in a life of drug addiction. As he was prayed for, he was set free instantly. God did it in a moment! And there were many other stories like it.

As the Holy Spirit ministered to people, many felt the effects on their physical bodies through tears, tremblings, outcries, bouts of laughter, or falling down. Some needed to be carried to a car, and some were driven home, as they were not physically able. Understandably, this brought many questions and concerns, particularly for those unfamiliar with the work of the Holy Spirit. But the church was cautioned not to judge these outward manifestations but rather to examine the fruit.

DRUNK IN THE HOLY SPIRIT

This move of God was not confined to church meetings alone. Personal Bible reading became alive, and many received fresh revelation during their time with the Lord.

Kay Weaver describes her experience this way. "Reflecting back over the years since the renewal in our church over 20 years ago, I would still say being drunk in the Holy Spirit was the best vacation I have ever had. I remember as our church was going through the renewal often praying that God would have His way in my life, and the renewal would produce fruit. About a month before being drunk in the Spirit, God brought me to a place of brokenness and surrender. I was the kind of person that didn't want life shaken up too much. Little did I know a big shaking was coming. I had a deep hunger and thirst for God over this time.

On the morning of November 8, 1994, I was praying to God that He would do whatever He needed to do in my life. That morning I was going to the hospital to visit a friend's son. As I arrived at the hospital, an overwhelming sense of peace, happiness, and joy overcame me. I started to laugh with uncontrollable joy as I drove around the parking lot. I literally felt lost in God's presence and couldn't think where to go. In the hospital I was overcome again with laughter. I walked into the patient's room full of the joy of the Lord. I don't know how I managed to drive home. God's presence was so powerful, I was not conscious of anything but Him. I tried calling my husband and some friends but just kept laughing on the phone. My husband said I sounded like a drunk that was intoxicated with alcohol. I remember that afternoon many different feelings of peace, joy, God's love, and compassion and love for others. God was giving me a heart for others.

A funny story over this time was going to the grocery store with a friend. Our youngest son was along, and I let him put whatever he wanted in the grocery cart, even the junky cereal I would normally not buy. When we got home I was too physically weak to put the groceries away and didn't even care about food over this time.

I continued drunk in the Spirit for three days, was physically weak, and could barely take care of home and family responsibilities. I spent most of my time in His presence as He spoke to me. He was doing a deep work in me and used that time to bring healing and a change in me for many things that were to come. As I prayed during the renewal for fruit to come, He brought many women into my life to minister to. I have been through many joys and some very dark days since then, but God has never let me go. He has been faithful and a good Father. Still, drunk in the Spirit was the greatest joy in my life."

The Wednesday night meetings were eventually moved to Friday nights. They were called Fresh Fire renewal meetings and were advertised as times of refreshing in the presence of the Lord. As God continued to pour out His Holy Spirit, many made new commitments to the Lordship of Jesus Christ. As word got out that God was moving in a new way, people desiring more of Him started coming from all over the region. With a purpose to serve the renewal in the region, Friday night meetings were made available to the whole community, as the church did not want to pull people away from their home churches on Sunday mornings. ECC enjoyed the time of fellowship as God brought people together from many different congregations and denominations. They believed that God was bringing a new level of unity to His church and breaking down walls that divided them. The Lord continued to surprise the church at these meetings by the way He radically changed lives in His presence.

THE RIVER OF LIFE

In 1995, as things with the renewal were increasing, the eldership team saw the value of setting aside two extended periods of time to seek God's face in addition to the weekly Friday night meetings. The vision was to provide additional opportunities for those who were thirsty to experience the current outpouring. These meetings were called "The River of Life" gatherings, one held in March and another in April of that year. The anointing and presence of God increased over the four nights of meetings. There were plenty of newcomers each evening, many returning several times and experiencing a deeper work of the Spirit each time. Several hundred guests from other congregations attended each evening.

But why call them "The River of Life?" While the church was

enjoying this outpouring, the question was about the larger purpose in all of it. Barry Wissler put things in perspective for the church. He shared about the vision of Ezekiel chapter 47, regarding a river of water coming from the presence of the Lord. Every place the river flowed, it brought life. The final destination of the river is the sea. As it flows into the sea, the waters of the sea become fresh and are filled with life. Barry taught that this sea is the sea of humanity or the lost multitudes of the world. Ezekiel records that fishermen will line the banks to spread their nets. The trees along the banks will bear fruit, and their leaves will be for healing. This vision speaks about the life of God going out to the lost. Therefore, this river of renewal must go to the lost. God was refreshing and renewing His church in preparation for a season of harvest! God was restoring intimacy with His church and rekindling their first love. God was manifesting His presence specifically to empower His people to reach the lost.

Barry Wissler often reminded the church that they get to keep what they give away, saying, "Whenever God is kind in blessing us, He wants us to extend His love and mercy to others. It is never just for us. In following the example of Jesus, we should lay down our lives for others and be willing to give away the life we receive. The Scriptures say that if we try to keep our life, we will lose it. But if we lose our life for His sake, we shall find it even more! Ask God to lead you in reaching out to others, whether they are unbelievers or other Christians who are thirsty. We have begun to see new conversions almost weekly, so although we can't call it a harvest yet, God is calling the lost, and the time is at hand to reap. Pray for the harvest and for the workers."

FRONT PAGE NEWS

In the spring of 1995, the press somehow found out about the renewal meetings. Without the knowledge of the leadership, they sent someone to a meeting to investigate. They were given permission to take some pictures, and later that weekend an article with photos ended up on the

Floored by the Spirit

Intelligencer Journal photo by Brian M. Christopher

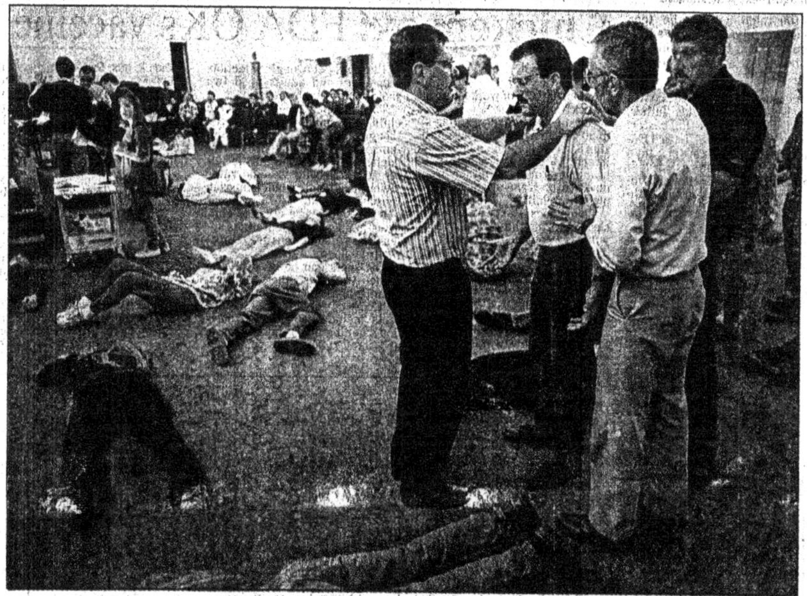

Newspaper article reports on the Renewal, spring 1995.

front page of Saturday morning's paper in full color. From that point, the renewal just exploded, and the meetings were packed full. People from all walks of life, including pastors, church people, and unbelievers, came to see what God was doing. Curiosity was mounting, and people wanted to experience this touch of God for themselves.

Word circulated about this move of God, and over 50 pastors from the area visited the church for prayer throughout these years. Some were wounded and came for a while to receive refreshment and healing and then returned to the ministry. This opened up the door to many relationships with other churches in the area. Previously, Ephrata Community Church had only related to the churches within the network. But during the renewal, they realized there were a lot of things happening in the body of Christ that they were not aware of and were out of touch with. Many local pastors began to partner with ECC in different areas and meetings. God, in His faithfulness, was expanding ECC's capacity for relationships and friendships in the region, in other states, and in other

countries. The church found themselves walking out their decision to become an Antioch church through resourcing the region with this outpouring.

By 1996, ECC was amazed that not only had the renewal continued to build locally, but it was also spreading around the world. The "Pensacola Outpouring" at Brownsville Assembly of God in Pensacola, Florida, had resulted in 20,000 commitments to Christ. Promise Keepers gathered 40,000 pastors and ministry leaders in Atlanta and was hailed as the largest gathering of clergy ever. And in Latin America, 40,000 Christians had filled a stadium in Cali, Colombia. These were only a few of the reports coming in from around the world.

RANDY CLARK

Considered to be one of the most significant events of the renewal for ECC was a week of meetings with Randy Clark. In early August 1996, Barry Wissler received a call that Randy Clark had an opening in his schedule and was available to come for a series of nightly meetings on a Monday through Saturday in September. With less than six weeks to prepare, ECC accepted the challenge with excitement. Randy was used by God to ignite the "Toronto Blessing" at Toronto Airport Christian Fellowship in Canada. To ECC, now a church of 200, it was an honor to be able to host Randy. Expecting possibly 1,000 or more people, ECC's church building was too small to contain the conference. DOVE Westgate of Ephrata graciously opened their church building to hold the meetings there. The desire of Barry and the elders was to hold some meetings in the area

Randy Clark spoke at "River of Life" meetings held nightly for a week at DOVE Westgate, September 9-14, 1996.

Congregational worship at the "River of Life" meetings, September 1996.

where a group of churches could come together to be refreshed in the presence of the Lord. For this series of meetings, they envisioned a group of local pastors linking together and working for widespread renewal in the region. And so the invitation was sent out, and 23 pastors responded with interest. The weeklong event was also called "The River of Life," taken from Ezekiel's vision.

Preparation began and an intercession team was put in place. Ushers, greeters, parking attendants, book and resource table staff were all recruited. Volunteers set up additional chairs to meet the attendance expectation of 1,000 people. A trained ministry team was organized to help pray for individuals during ministry times. Randy brought along his worship leader, Gary Shelton. Gary was one of the main worship leaders for the St. Louis Vineyard Church and was particularly anointed in playing guitar and leading the church into the presence of God. God had used him powerfully as he led worship in the renewal meetings at the Toronto Airport Christian Fellowship.

God showed up in miraculous ways that week. The anticipation of experiencing God's presence filled the room every night. Each evening, Gary Shelton would lead worship for about an hour, followed by a time of testimonies. Randy Clark would preach, and at the conclusion of the message, all the chairs were removed and stacked to make room for the many who came forward for personal ministry. Gary would lead worship for hours as Randy and the ministry team ministered to individuals.

Ministry would go into the early morning. On one particular night, the leadership team did not leave until three o'clock in the morning. No one tired of this, as the presence of God was so evident in sustaining people during this time. It was difficult for many to leave His presence and return home. Some had traveled from out of state to experience what God was doing. Friday night was youth night, and the room was filled with hungry youth anticipating God's touch. The hunger for more of God's presence was also evident in the sales of worship CDs and books. Between the material that Randy and Gary brought along and the material ECC had available, almost $6,000 worth were sold during those six days! And during 1996 alone, the ECC bookstore sold over $14,000 in books and CDs produced by renewal speakers and musicians.

FANNING THE FLAME

As hunger grew in the region for more of God, many outside renewal speakers were invited to hold conferences similar to the one with Randy Clark. These outside speakers continued to spur the renewal, and the meetings continued to pack out for each conference. Some of the speakers invited were Joseph and Barbara Garlington, Fred Grewe, Graham Cooke from England, Mark and Susie Roye, Marc Dupont, David and Kathy Walters, Rick and Annie Stivers, Richard and Glenda Holcomb, Mark Sandford, Larry Randolph, Marcelo Diaz from Argentina, and others. Each brought different elements to the renewal. Graham Cooke prophesied that Ephrata Community Church would become a "resource church," unaware that they had already adopted the Antioch model of church. This was yet another confirmation of the church's calling to the region and beyond. It also confirmed a vision of a network of churches and ministries partnering together for the harvest, which was in the birthing stage at that point.

HEAVEN TOUCHED EARTH

One particularly memorable experience happened on Saturday night, May 30, 1998, with speaker Jim Goll. Later, Barry Wissler described it this way, "I have never experienced anything like it. Heaven and earth seemed to overlap. This incredible time of worship lasted only about 45 minutes but has been labeled by many to be an all-time high point of their experience of the presence of God. Jim's teaching on intercession was very motivational all weekend, but after his message Saturday night, he suggested that we go back into worship for a while. And then it happened. There was explosive and sponta-

Mark Ulrich led worship for many hours during ministry time throughout the Renewal, ca. 1997.

neous worship and then a period of intense silence. I have been in a lot of great meetings over the years but never have I felt that heaven was so close to breaking out on earth as that night. This was just a foretaste of the kind of presence God wants to deposit in our region. I believe that God wants (and so do we!) a sustained habitation of His presence. Intercession and worship will play a major role in building an altar on which God can descend and inhabit. Jim told us that before a break-through there arises a people who declare what is not, as though it were."

Mark Ulrich was leading the song, Be Magnified, and began to repeat the chorus over and over as worship began to explode. As he felt heaven touching earth and the holy presence of God filling the room, he could not continue. Drummer Don Weber fell on his face on the floor in God's holy presence, acknowledging his worthlessness before the holiness of God. Don felt he could not get low enough on the floor as he experienced God's holiness. He had never felt anything like that before and hasn't since. Many in the room had similar experiences during the time of intense silence that night.

PROPHETIC PRAYER AND INTERCESSION

One of the most encouraging developments during the renewal was the

CELEBRATING 40 YEARS OF GOD'S FAITHFULNESS

number of individuals who were called to intercede and pray. Out of this burden to pray, God birthed what has been called "prophetic intercession." This is intercession led by the Holy Spirit with a prophetic-like anointing. The church was encouraged to seek God's heart and will so that the things that move Him would move them. As they would pray God's will, the power of the Kingdom of God would break forth into action. The church was encouraged to be open to God's direction toward the harvest. While the church was personally enjoying the refreshing, it was ultimately God's heart for the church to focus on a harvest of the lost. They were encouraged to pray that the harvest would be prepared and He would send out workers into the fields.

With a renewed focus on worship and intercession, the Friday night meetings transitioned to "The Watch" meetings. As the church hungered for a harvest of lost souls, it understood that one of the primary ways for the church to do spiritual warfare was through worship and intercession. Revival would be a result of God's work and not the church's. Intercession would surely hasten revival. ECC decided to join the more than 200 churches around the nation holding "Watch of the Lord" meetings. The focus was to come together to spend the night with the Lord and hear the sound of His call. The nights were spent in worship, intercession, and waiting on God. A ministry team continued to offer ministry to individuals as the Lord led.

FRESH FIRE YOUTH MINISTRY

The youth at ECC were also impacted by the renewal. Beginning with only 18, the small group soon mushroomed to 80 youth, with half attending from other churches. The youth became involved in all aspects of ministry, while still attending their own churches. As the ECC youth embraced those from other churches, they also began to walk out the church's calling as an Antioch church. Under the direction of youth pastors, Mark and Marlene Ulrich, they chose the name Fresh Fire Youth Ministry to reflect more than a local church youth group.

As God changed their lives, the teens grew spiritually by leaps

Youth hungry for more of the Holy Spirit filled the barn on Sunday nights, ca. 1996.

and bounds. Their hunger for God challenged those around them to examine their priorities. Their prayers filled the room and ascended to the throne of Jesus. In prayer, they called down power and anointing in their meetings, cried out for the lost in their schools, and asked for strongholds to be broken and peers to be free. They would pray fervently, often making it difficult for others to interject with their prayers.

It was written about the youth during the renewal:
You know it's God when…
- A teenager prays "turn our parties into prayer meetings"
- Youth arrive ½ hour before a prayer meeting and begin praying
- Youth arrange their own prayer meetings on Friday evenings
- Youth "swarm" the youth leaders with prayer
- Youth confess hidden sins and are set free
- Youth ask for "God's heart for the lost"

The youth meetings consisted of worship, led by one of three youth worship bands, a time for testimonies, and teaching from the Word. At the conclusion of the meeting, a call for ministry was given, which was often met with an overwhelming response. As the youth ministered in prayer for each other, God's love was lavished on them, and their lives were changed.

Overnight bus trips were taken to Toronto Christian Fellowship to attend their renewal youth conferences. One such trip was reminiscent of what happened in the '70s among the church founders. God sovereignly poured out His Spirit on the teens, seizing their hearts for Himself. It was radical and wonderful to watch as new passion for Jesus was ignited in their hearts. They spent eight hours praying on the drive home, weeping and crying out for their lost friends and asking God for His heart and power to save them.

Another trip was taken to the Elisha Generation Youth Conference in Brownsville, Florida to experience a similar movement of God. Mark and Marlene Ulrich, assisted by Don and Karen Weber and Rich and Betty Petersheim, often stood in amazement at the hand of God moving among the youth.

WHY EPHRATA COMMUNITY CHURCH?

Of all the places across the region where God could have done this work, why did He choose this seemingly insignificant, small country church? At ECC, in spite of their weaknesses, He found a people who loved God and deeply desired to know Him. They had a willingness to

Youth traveled to Pensacola, Florida to attend a conference.

make adjustments and to accommodate what was happening in order to fully welcome this move of God. From their beginning days together, the group always carried a sense of adventure and a heart to share it with others who were willing to join them. The heart that connected those 12 people in the 1970s was still present and strong some 20 years later. God was invited there, and He showed up in a significant way. In His sovereignty and goodness, God chose the congregation of Ephrata Community Church.

During the renewal years, ECC certainly felt that they had received a visitation of God. Many Christians and churches in the area had been awakened and renewed by the outpouring of the Holy Spirit in the region. But while they enjoyed this visitation, their heart's desire was for a sustained habitation. A visitation usually lasts a few years and then subsides, as the renewal eventually did. Some blamed the leadership for the end of this move of God. But the visitation was just that—a visit from God, which was powerful and transformative—but not permanent. The church had opened the door and had welcomed the Holy Spirit for a length of time. And as they continued to pursue Him, the desire increased for a sustained habitation, where God would move in and stay among them.

While the renewal was a positive event in the life of the church, it also brought a big transition. The small, conservative, charismatic church had to process what God was doing because they had never seen or experienced anything like it before. The outpouring of the Holy Spirit provided a supernatural power to the church to further their outreach in the region.

Throughout the renewal, attendance had skyrocketed and the meeting room in the church was continually packed. Every possible space was filled with chairs, and the aisles were so narrow that passing others was difficult. After several overflow meetings, the elders added a second service on Saturday nights. The vision for the Saturday night meeting was to reach new people who were unable or unlikely to attend a Sunday meeting. Both meetings were fully staffed church services, including classes for the children. Some families serving or attending the Saturday night service saw their role as an outreach to others. Holding two services was a stretch for the church that enjoyed fellowshipping and being together for all corporate gatherings. But they also acknowledged that an additional service was needed to reach more people.

THE BIRTH OF HARVESTNET

"Mend the nets!" was a word the Lord spoke to Barry Wissler shortly after the renewal broke out in 1994. The word was about God forming a large net for the harvest. God revealed to Barry that He wanted to use relationships as a net to reach the lost. Mending the nets involved strengthening every kind of relationship from marriages and families to friendships within the church body. But especially crucial were the relationships between churches. God was building new connections and partnerships between churches and ministries for the work of the harvest. A new God-breathed love and trust among the various parts of the Body of Christ was knitting the net together. Churches and ministries that at one time worked independently were finding one another and realizing their shared vision for revival and harvest.

With the planting of Covenant Community Church, HarvestNet was initially born to help foster a partnering relationship between the two congregations. But God's plan was much larger. Two more congregations were planted in 1999; Willow Street Community Church and Boanerges in Palmyra. Numerous other connections were formed by friendships between pastors and churches during the renewal meetings, and the tiny network began to grow.

In 1997, Graham Cooke's prophetic word confirmed the role of Ephrata Community Church as a "resource church." ECC soon realized that God wanted to do more than build a local church. He wanted to birth a ministry that would provide resources to develop and strengthen local churches and ministries. ECC had already embraced the vision of being a sending and planting church, so the word brought by Cooke was one of expanding the vision for developing and providing resources.

Soon Ephrata Community Church and HarvestNet became interwoven in a partnership and began to host conferences with outside ministries to teach and equip churches of the region for revival. Because of the great need to train workers for the harvest, they also planned training opportunities like The School of the Spirit and the Elijah House Counselor Training. Leadership gatherings and training events were designed specifically to foster relationships, promote revival, and equip churches.

The most exciting part of HarvestNet's work was linking people together for the mission of harvest. Whether it was for local outreach or for foreign missions, they understood that these tasks would be accomplished best when efforts and resources were joined. They envisioned a new level of unity and teamwork as churches would join together in prayer and begin to trust one another. They believed this was the foundation for a sustained habitation of God's presence in the region. The harvest of God would require churches and ministries to work together. There became a growing awareness that there was really only one church in our region—the larger body of Christ. Although leaders and pastors were accountable to and cared for their own individual churches, they were also linked together into one regional body.

HarvestNet desired to do its part in blessing and strengthening the "regional church." And so it became an informal relational network of churches and ministries, linked together by a shared vision and a desire to partner in the coming harvest. The goal was to build by relationships and not by structure. The belief of a great harvest coming and the work being accomplished best through partnership became the fuel and foundation for HarvestNet. Their central love of the presence of God was reflected in their commitment to worship, corporate prayer, and the ministry of the Holy Spirit—all resulting in a people zealous to serve the Lord for revival. Their approach to missions included evangelism, spiritual warfare, unity among churches, intergenerational ministry, and a commitment to heal the wounded.

Even though the renewal was dying down, like tornados that often spin off a hurricane, so the renewal also spun off ministries. Out of the partnership between Ephrata Community Church and HarvestNet, several multi-church ministries were birthed under HarvestNet's banner. ECC became the "resource church," which connected the family of churches and ministries together relationally. They created an atmosphere of warm hospitality for conferences, where speakers and guests felt welcome.

BREATH OF LIFE MINISTRIES

During the many hours of ministry to individuals, Ephrata Community Church became acutely aware of the desperate needs of hurting people. While many people were miraculously healed and set free instantly, there were others still in need of additional ministry. God began placing a desire in the hearts of some believers to be trained to offer personal ministry at a deeper level.

Elijah House was a worldwide ministry that presented seminars, lectures, workshops, counseling courses, and prayer ministry training across denominational boundaries. This ministry seemed like a good fit, with their focus on training lay counselors. In October 1997, 65 students from 21 different churches began an intensive, 19-week Elijah House Training for the Ministry of Prayer Counseling. Cindy Smith facilitated the video school. The students interacted and studied together for the purpose of being equipped with some powerful tools to help minister to those with deep hurts.

While working through the 6-month program, God began to stir the hearts of several leaders with a vision for a prayer counseling ministry to be established in the region. It was an exciting process, as the ideas and dreams of many people were knit together into what became Breath of Life Ministries in October 1998, with Rob Stoppard as the director. The name was birthed from the word "revive," which means "breathe new life into." The purpose of this ministry was to help facilitate restoration and reconciliation within the church body, in families, and in the community using Elijah House and other biblically based counseling principles and Holy Spirit-directed prayer counseling. A pool of trained prayer counselors became committed to the task of restoring broken relationships and bringing healing to the hurt and wounded in the name of Jesus Christ. The ministry was birthed not only out of a desire to provide biblical counseling and healing to those who were hurting but to also enable multiple churches to share counselor training and resources in accomplishing the task.

Word began to spread about the prayer counseling ministry. Along with clients calling for sessions, several calls a week were received from pastors inquiring about the ministry. They were looking for help with failing marriages, children/youth in crisis, and parenting issues within their congregation. In addition to prayer counseling, BOLM also began to offer Elijah House basic video schools, seminars, and training for counselors. To accommodate the need for counseling rooms and offices, the unused space of the ECC office building was renovated to provide a non-threatening, confidential atmosphere for counseling.

Dr. Loren McRae became the director in 2003, followed by Sue Ferrari in 2010. Sue remains the current director. While the ministry dealt with the typical issues of stress, anger, depression, and anxiety, Sue's directorship helped to expand into abuse and addiction, grief and loss, and employer/employee issues. These new ministry areas required more specialized training. As the Holy Spirit continued to transform lives, BOLM was invited to minister to women in prison, ex-offenders in residential transitional programs, and those with intellectual and developmental disabilities. They also provided inner healing to residential clients in a local rescue mission.

Many individuals found the freedom and the healing they needed as counselors gently guided them in the power of the Holy Spirit. One client testified, "I'll be honest, my life was headed downhill fast. I was severely depressed, making poor decisions and had lost touch with God. I needed help. At Breath of Life, I received the spiritual guidance I needed to get my life back on track. Many of my problems stemmed from childhood and family issues. Through counseling, I learned the principles of sowing and reaping. I learned how to forgive...and mean it. I was taught how to give my burdens to God, not keep them stuffed inside! My life is much different now. I now talk with God on a daily basis. My depression lifted, and my physical health improved. Now when I am faced with an adversity, I can honestly say, 'The Lord is with me, and we will get through this!' I count my blessings every day, and this ministry team is definitely a blessing in my life!"

BOLM eventually became their own non-profit entity and opened offices in Ephrata and Lancaster. In the 19 years since its founding, it is estimated that between the two locations, they have ministered to over 7,500 individuals! This ministry was birthed out of the Antioch church model of resourcing the region and continues today to serve the desperate and hurting in significant ways.

TIMES OF TESTING—TIMES OF ADVANCEMENT

FRAGMENTED LEADERSHIP

From 1997-1999, God allowed the church to enter into a very important and difficult phase of transition and preparation, testing the church many times. The work of the Holy Spirit had not stopped. It was just going deeper and looked different. God was taking His work much deeper than the church was expecting. His methods and timetables were different from theirs. They realized their part in the process was to embrace what God was doing and to continue their intercession and worship to their great God. And He would fulfill all that He had promised.

The renewal had run fairly strong for about three years and then began to slow down, in terms of healings and other manifestations not being as frequent. After transitioning the Friday night gatherings to intercession meetings, the attendance shrank to about 125 on those evenings. Barry Wissler and the eldership team were never interested in perpetuating something that had run its course. Eventually, the Friday night meetings were stopped.

One area affected during this new phase of transition was the church leadership. Several things contributed to a fragmentation, or breakdown, in the leadership team. After 14 years of providing oversight, the relationship between ECC and Ray Ciervo of New Covenant Ministries dissolved in 1995. While Barry Wissler had been functioning as the lead elder, another three elders had been assisting him in leading the church. Towards the end of the renewal, two of the elders felt that their time in leadership at ECC was drawing to a close. The church found themselves in a position with only two elders remaining, Barry Wissler and Mark Ulrich.

As Barry felt the weight of the leadership team fragmenting—one that had been strong since the start of the church—he was weary and just wanted to quit. After writing his letter of resignation, he and his family packed their bags and were prepared to leave the area for several days. But before they could leave the house, Leon Price called Barry on the phone and said, "Barry, what is going on up there?" God had given Leon a prophetic sense that the church was in trouble. After spending two hours on the phone with Leon, Barry realized quitting was not an option, and he tore up his resignation letter. A godly prophetic figure loving on them, comforting them, guiding them, and cheering them on was found in Leon Price. God used his servant, Leon, to stabilize the church during that shaky season.

As the leadership transitioned, it became a difficult and confusing time for those attending the church, and many were tested at a deep level. But they prayed and held to the vision that they were a people pursuing God to see His Kingdom come on the earth. Their God brought them through this far and was faithful and able to take them onward!

The church was not in a position to choose new elders at that time, so the Advisory Council was established to help carry the responsibility of making decisions. This group consisted of those carrying some form of responsibility within the congregation. Their role was to provide an informal forum between the elders and the congregation.

FATHER IN THE HOUSE—ALAN VINCENT

With the strength of an eldership team faltering, Barry Wissler and the congregation were in need of someone outside of the church who could bring some stability, direction, and oversight. Alan Vincent, whom the church had met years earlier, was passing through the area and asked Barry to lunch. As Barry shared the church's struggles, Alan provided wisdom and insight to help them. This divine encounter was the seed

Alan and Eileen Vincent, 1999.

for what would become a long and significant relationship. Barry asked Alan Vincent to come and speak to the church at a revival and worship service in late October 1998. Alan had a wealth of experience, with sensitivity to the Holy Spirit and a deep-rooted faith. Along with his wife, Eileen, they had traveled extensively and spoke from firsthand experience of the work of God in Eastern

Europe, Africa, and Asia. They had spent 13 years serving in India as missionaries, during which they received the baptism of the Holy Spirit and saw thousands saved and many churches established. Originally from England, they had moved their ministry, Outpouring Ministries, to San Antonio, Texas. They served a growing network of leaders and churches in North and Central America, as well as continuing their travel to India and various countries in Europe and Africa.

Almost immediately, there was a supernatural connection established between Alan and ECC. Once again, God was faithful to provide in a time of need and brought Alan to Ephrata Community Church at just the right time. Alan visited the church on six weekends in the first six months, sometimes with his wife, Eileen. The church was hungry for Alan's teachings on grace and faith, imparting a depth of expectancy in God that the church had not yet experienced. Eileen imparted a revelation of the power of intercession into the church. In those first few months, as the relationship between Alan and the church deepened, it became clearly evident that God had sent Alan to ECC for a larger purpose. Alan accepted the invitation to oversee the church and become a spiritual father to Barry. While a board of elders would govern ECC, Alan would advise and speak into the overall life and vision of the church.

With only two functioning elders, Alan began to help Barry rebuild a team of leaders. Alan spent time interviewing prospective elders. With the agreement of the existing elders and consensus of the congregation, three more elders were ordained and installed in June 1999. Kevin Eshleman, Ivan Martin, and Glenn Weaver became part of the eldership team joining Mark Ulrich and Barry Wissler in leading the church forward. They recognized their unique blend of giftings and perspectives and were committed to working together to advance the kingdom. Stephanie Eshleman, Rosene Martin, and Kay Weaver acknowledged the calling on their husbands' lives and stood with them in their ordination.

Alan Vincent was a perfect fit in helping ECC to refine their focus as an equipping, resource church. He confirmed the church's calling

79

Elder ordination of Kevin Eshleman, Ivan Martin & Glenn Weaver
(From left: Kevin & Stephanie Eshleman, Alan & Eileen Vincent, Rosene & Ivan
Martin, Kay & Glenn Weaver) June 6, 1999.

and the work of HarvestNet. Alan remained for many years as the most
prominent leader speaking into the church. His involvement gradually
lessened in later years as his health declined.

IN THE MIDST OF TURMOIL, GOD MOVES MIGHTILY

Even as the church wrestled with leadership transitions, God continued
to move in powerful ways. In hindsight, God used those three years to
put into motion His greater vision for the church.

Eileen Vincent was well known for her anointing in the area of
intercession, as she had been able to mobilize thousands of intercessors to
pray for the San Antonio region. With prayer and intercession already in
the DNA of the church, Eileen came to equip and motivate the church
to intercede for the region. The call to war in the spiritual realm had been
clear. The time was right for the church to intensify their prayer efforts
for revival in the region and the state. Responding to the importance
of prayer, a group of intercessors was put in place as a prayer shield for
Barry and Cheryl Wissler and the church for protection and guidance.

Numerous prophetic and apostolic sources called the church forth to intercede, which resulted in corporate prayer meetings, 30 Days of Prayer and Fasting, and Watch of the Lord meetings, some of which lasted all night long. Jim Goll led a conference called "Watchmen, Gatekeepers, and Warriors," where he imparted the power of intercession, prophetic ministry, and life in the Spirit.

Many felt the word from God for the year 1998 was to rebuild the altar of the Lord. The three-strand cord of intercession, worship, and the prophetic would create a place for the sustained habitation of the Lord. God was issuing a call to prayer and intercession. In the Old Testament, the priests were instructed to never let the fire on the altar go out. As priests of the New Covenant, the church felt they should give themselves no rest and not keep silent, but rather remind the Lord day and night of His promises until they are fulfilled. God was setting things in motion for His future plans for intercession in the region.

During this time, God also began to call His daughters to rise and take their place in the church. As the elders of ECC recognized what God was doing among women, they saw the need to appoint a team to minister to and encourage them. Covering them with prayer and blessing, the leadership released the women of the church into all that God had in store for them. The women saw the need to step up and take the places that God had called them to and to be equipped together through meetings and retreats to fulfill their destiny in God.

MOVE TO DOVE WESTGATE BUILDING

The renewal had brought many people to the church. Some were new converts, and others were looking to experience more of the Holy Spirit. In one year, the size of the church had more than doubled, and the leadership began to seriously talk about building a church building. In 1997, the first building committee was gathered together. The church had added a Saturday night service, which was totally different from the Sunday service. It felt like the church had become two separate congregations. The eldership team wasn't comfortable with what was

Worship team at DOVE Westgate, 1997.

happening. In March 1997, after entering into an agreement to share worship facilities with DOVE Westgate and Pastor Duane Britton, Ephrata Community Church moved both services to Saturday night at the Westgate building, which was about three miles east along Route 322. This plan was meant to only last a year, while they decided where to build and to draw up building plans.

It was a big transition to meet on Saturday nights for a church used to Sunday morning meetings. During this time at Westgate, the church celebrated their 20th anniversary, which included baptizing 59 believers during the anniversary weekend. It was a time of rejoicing and celebration. The church also launched out two groups of people to plant churches. Boanerges Christian Fellowship met in Palmyra, pastored by Kent Perry, and Willow Street Community Church met in Kendig Square, pastored by Frank Ferrari. After 10 months of meeting at Westgate and with about 100 fewer people as a result of the church plants, the church returned to the barn on the ECC campus.

The congregation knew this was only a temporary arrangement. They believed that a solution to their facility dilemma would become clear as they continued to focus on the harvest of the lost. They knew the harvest was where God was taking them, and they desired to fully cooperate with all He wanted to do in preparation. In the meantime,

Congregational worship at DOVE Westgate facilities, 1997.

they would continue to pursue options and would add multiple services if it became necessary.

As the church continued to grow, Barry felt the need for additional help in pastoring the church, and Mark Ulrich was hired as an Associate Pastor in January 1999. In April of that year, the church began holding two services on Sunday mornings. And by September, a congregational meeting was held to inform the members of the building committee findings and to discuss the possibility of a new building.

IF YOU BUILD IT, THEY WILL COME

On October 31, 1999, the Lord spoke a prophetic word through Marc Dupont that provided much encouragement and confirmation for many years to come.

"I feel that the Lord has told me this about this church. What is happening in the natural is also going to take place in the supernatural. That you are to build this building and even though there's been several years of turmoil in the church, the Lord is saying that's been foundational for what's to come. I know the church is not a brand new church, but

Marc Dupont prophesied, "If you build it, they will come," October 31, 1999.

you've been going through almost an adolescent period with the vision, the call, and the gifts that God's placed upon this church. There's been high energy, there's been passion, but God has been grounding more wisdom into the leaders and into the church.

I'm not familiar with farming and farming terminology and all that, but I saw what you call a silo, a big spiritual silo going up in this place, very tall one. And the Lord said He's going to fill this silo with worship going to heaven and prayers spilling out. And just as the Lord told Joseph when he got to Egypt and came into that place of authority to build and store for seven years, and there was going to be a famine and they were going to have enough to pour out for the whole nation. The Lord didn't tell me there was going to be a famine upon this area. He's not speaking about food anyway. He's speaking about spiritual food. But God is saying you're about to go into a seven-year period of growth and storing up and storing up prayer and worship. And growing and growing and growing, especially you're going to grow in the ability to worship God. I felt like the Lord was saying that He's going to bring other people to the church as well that are gifted and called for intercessory prayer and worship.

Let me give a word of encouragement to some of you. Sometimes we have our fixed little positions and then God upsets the apple cart by bringing something new. Don't try to fight for position or things like that, because God always has something better for you. And you know when Jesus said to Peter that I think there's going to be a martyr, and then Peter turns around and points and says, 'What about him?' And Jesus says, 'Don't worry about him. You do what's on for you.' (John 21:18–21) If God brings some people to the church that are more gifted in the area of ministry that you've been responsible for, you've been part of something, just make room for them because it doesn't belong to you anyway. But if you let it go, it'll just come back to you, pressed down in good measure. I'm just saying this because sometimes we think this is church, this is your ministry, this is my ministry. You and I don't really have ministry, all ministry belongs to the Holy Spirit. We're just fellow coworkers with Him.

I think there's going to come a fresh release of creativity to the church as far as worship, a birthing of creativity from within. I also believe there's going to be a new momentum of prayer, and what Jesus said, the two primary things that God always looks for in the church, there is going to be a whole new thing taking place here in worship. But also this is going to become more and more a house of prayer, not just intercessory prayer but prophetic prayer and worship prayer. God has some things in store for you as far as prayer that your eyes have not seen and your ears have not heard and has not entered your understanding.

I believe there's going to be continual evangelism happening. I think there's going to be steady growth, and there is going to be evangelism, but you're to build. Not only physically, but spiritually. You're going to grow and grow in seven years, and then there's going to be an explosion of the things God is building. This silo filled up of worship and prayer is just going to explode out of here. You remember that old Kevin Costner movie "Field of Dreams," where he builds that baseball diamond out in the cornfields and the voice came to him and that so-called message he had, 'If you build it, they will come.' I feel like the Lord is saying to you that now is the time to build.

I know some of you feel, well, we've gone through problems and there's been this shaking and that shaking. Shall we just stay where we're at? But see in the Kingdom of God, either things are going forward or going backward. There's no middle ground. This is a time for sowing. This is time for sowing into the Spirit; this is time for sowing into buildings; this is time for sowing into yourselves, seeking God, and it will come back to you, pressed down in good measure, and to build this building, and the Lord will fill it, and it will be a place of resource.

Worship-wise, I don't know the time and season, but I see in the Spirit the Tabernacle of David being established here. I don't know what God's timing is, but I believe you're going to have all-night sessions of worship and prayer. I believe this church is going to go on to be a worship resource center and prayer resource center for many other churches in this area and this region. He's about to do something and His presence and His glory is going to be found here by many, many hurting, desperate people."

(4)

BUILDING FOR THE
HARVEST 2000 – 2014

WHY BUILD?

After several years of turmoil and change, the church felt comfortable meeting back in the barn again with the dream of a new building growing in their hearts. God continued to add to their numbers during this time, and in less than a year, the meeting room was packed once again. They responded by adding another Sunday morning service, while the building committee began developing plans and starting the long process of land development.

The question at that time was, "Why build?" God clearly told Barry Wissler that the church would receive the church building that God wanted if they focused on the harvest. The challenge was to build for the harvest. God has promised a tremendous end-time harvest in His Word, and it would need to be housed someplace. The bigger the harvest, the bigger the "barns" would need to be. ECC wanted to be prudent and do its part, both to reap the harvest and to house it. Their only goal was to build a "barn" big enough to hold the share of the harvest that God wanted to bring their way. At the time, they had no more capacity for growth.

The church was about to engage in a much needed building campaign. It was becoming apparent that a major transition needed to happen to take them from a local church with a kind of small-town mentality to a full regional center with an apostolic team serving the region and the nations. What would this building look like? How would they pay for it? Two years after commissioning a building committee to begin the process, the congregation unanimously voted to move forward with the project.

FUNDING THE BUILDING PROJECT

Ten acres of land, adjacent to the barn, was generously donated. With $813,000 already in the bank, the elders presented a plan for investing in the harvest. "Not equal giving, but equal sacrifice" became their tagline. Building for the harvest would go beyond paying for a building. Their sacrificial giving would turn into blessings for many years. With a new building, there were many new ministry opportunities on the horizon, including youth and children's ministry, a café for fellowship, outreach events for the community, the hiring of additional staff, and the space to host HarvestNet events and larger conferences.

To make it work, it would take faith, togetherness, spiritual decision-making, involvement, sacrifice, and systematic giving. While the building committee worked through all the preparation and plans, church members accepted the challenge to seek God for their part in financing the project. One thing was clear to all—ministry would continue and would receive the same financial resources while they saved for the building.

RESTORATION OF THE TABERNACLE OF DAVID

Having come through a season of renewal and now entering a building project, the Lord introduced the church to a different kind of "building model." For 25 years, the church talked about intercession, worship, healing, deliverance, evangelism, unity, harvest, and spiritual warfare. And while they saw some progress in those areas, they had still fallen short of the kind of power and momentum they needed to really see them come into fullness. Restoring the Tabernacle of David was their answer. Like David, without the manifest presence of God in their midst, their efforts would yield only meager results. Alan Vincent taught that a Tabernacle of David would become the powerhouse behind transforming lives in the region.

According to 1 Chronicles, chapters 15–17, the Tabernacle of David was basically a tent. This tent housed the ark of God, where the presence of God rested. Anyone could come and meet with God in the tent. There were no barriers, and both Jews and Gentiles were welcome. There was no outer court, inner court, or holy of holies, and no veil separating the people from the actual presence of God. There were worshippers and musicians who worshipped God 24 hours a day, seven days a week. It was a place of extravagant worship, a place of prayer, and a place of unhindered access to God himself. People were healed and blessed as they came to meet with God. Out of this God-filled tent, the kingdom grew in strength and unity, and God's people enjoyed a period of unprecedented righteousness, peace, and prosperity. This is what Jesus referred to in Matthew 21:13 when He talked about His house being a house of prayer. He was talking about the restoration of the Tabernacle of David. If Ephrata Community Church could build a spiritual house that was attractive to God, He would release His manifest presence to fill the house. As the prophetic word encouraged, "If you build it, He will come."

Barry shared with the church that the ultimate purpose of rebuilding David's Tabernacle was for evangelism, as it would be a place to bring both the presence of God and evangelism together. Throughout history, wherever a Tabernacle of David was raised up and the presence of God came, the purpose was simply to bring the multitudes into the kingdom. Barry challenged the church to pursue God through worship and prayer and to pursue the harvest through evangelism. Both would need to be done simultaneously to achieve God's purposes.

In Psalm 132, David dreamed of a temple that was inhabited by God's presence. He sang of it, prayed for it, planned for it, recruited workers for it, supervised it; and eventually, a house was built for the Lord. Barry encouraged the church that they too can be builders who prepare and can build a place for the Lord to inhabit right in Ephrata.

Ephrata was named after the town Ephrathah (also called Bethlehem) in Psalm 132. A little town, out of the way, which became a place of fruitfulness, a place of birth. God uses little places to mightily bless the world. Ephrata was named by Christians and dedicated as a place of fruitfulness. Ephrata Community Church took on that identity as a people who longed for a habitation of God on the earth. Barry encouraged the church to be a people who would not rest until they saw the "ark presence" of God manifested. A people who will not only long for it, hope for it, pray for it, believe for it, but also work for it. David did all of those things in preparation, but he also did the work of building a house for the Lord. The church was encouraged to do the same. The content of Psalm 132 became the dream of Ephrata Community Church. They were to build a house for God, a place of prayer, claiming His promises.

There was a hunger in the community for God and a belief that as He would fill His church with His presence, unprecedented numbers would come to Christ. During this time, many other churches also heard God's call to build larger buildings than they currently needed simply because of the great needs of the coming harvest. The prophetic word "If you build it, they will come" became a promise and stirred them to move forward.

CHILDREN'S MINISTRY

As ECC was preparing to build a physical building, God was preparing the congregation in other ways. By the year 2000, after 23 years, the children's ministry had evolved from a total of 1 infant to approximately

Children's ministry, 1988.

35 children, ranging from nursery through grade 6. Over the years, as children were added to the church, a nursery and age-appropriate classes were formed. Curriculum was ordered and taught by volunteers. In the early years, a mobile classroom was added to the rear of the barn to accommodate additional classes. The children joined their parents in the service for a time of multigenerational, corporate praise and worship before being dismissed to classes during the message.

In 1999, Ivan and Rosene Martin, assisted by Ray and Patti Good, began a children's church for grades 1–6. This was initially for the first service and then eventually added for the second service, as well. The number of children continued to grow, and the elders soon appointed Ivan Martin as the first children's pastor in January 2000, so that he could give specialized care and pastoral support to the children and teachers. The church found excellent curriculum from Willie George Ministries to support their teaching. With the installation of a children's pastor, something shifted spiritually, signaling the value and importance of children in the church. A children's ministry was established, not to take the responsibility from training in the home, but rather to support it.

Children worshipping at kids' camp.

While the staff taught the stories in the Bible, they also taught the children that God had not stopped doing miracles. The same Jesus that healed the sick in the Bible also heals today, and they could know Him personally. The goal was to bring the children into an experience with the Lord. They were taught that there was no junior Holy Spirit. This became the DNA of the children's ministry. As children and youth, they were able to do whatever their parents were doing. The children were taught that the Lord wanted to speak and flow through them in the same way as He did with the adults. With the goal of leading each child into a personal relationship with the Lord, the team introduced regular Bible reading, prayer, and memory verse programs.

KIDS' CAMP

One day while Ivan Martin was mowing in his meadow, he received a vision from the Lord of a possible kids' camp for the ministry. After finding a location at the Mt. Airy Picnic Woods, and with Dale and Jackie Martin recruiting and managing a food service team, the first kids' summer camp was held June 18–21, 2000. It was a rustic setting, with 34 children sleeping in tents, using outhouses, and meeting in temporary facilities. After a few years and with the children's ministry growing, a larger and more accommodating facility was found at Refreshing Mountain Camp. The kids' camp eventually grew to 150 kids as a more evangelistic emphasis was made.

First kids' camp at Mt. Airy Picnic Woods, 2000.

One memorable year, Don Weber gave a prophecy that the Lord would pour out His Spirit on the children at kids' camp. That year many children experienced the touch of the Holy Spirit and spent extended times in worship, prayer, and waiting in the presence of the Lord rather than rushing off to meals. Over the years, it has always been a highlight for ECC to watch children begin relationships with Jesus, get baptized, and be supplied with Bibles and resource materials to help in their new walk with the Lord.

As the Lord led the elders in new directions and added to their vision, it always permeated the rest of the church. Children's ministry was no different. As the church began to focus outward and into missions, the children's ministry did the same. They received offerings to sponsor school students in other countries. The focus was to look past themselves to others. On various mission trips hosted by the church, some of the children actually met those that they were sponsoring. The seed was being planted to reach the nations. Providing a tangible way for the children to give to the nations, the children's ministry has sponsored Operation Christmas Child for the past 10 years.

Ivan and Rosene had volunteered their time for 11 years, but with a third service on the horizon, they felt the grace lifting to continue volunteering in the same capacity. Under their leadership, the ministry

Kids Camp, 2010.

had grown from 35 children to approximately 200. The elders decided it was time to make the transition from a volunteer position to a hired children's pastor. In March 2011, Jesse Rothacker was hired part-time as the children's pastor for several years, followed by Neil Beatty.

Over the years, the children's ministry has become one of the draws for quite a few families with young children. Often they visit and return because their children enjoy the children's ministry. The connections that the children make each week often become a foundation for relationships that last through youth ministry. The connections in children's ministry are so strong that many sixth graders are reluctant to leave it for youth ministry.

Presently in 2017, children's ministry involves 145 volunteers who minister to 375 children from infant nursery through grade six. Through all the years and transitions, God's faithfulness has been evident as His Word had flowed down from the leadership, through the teachers, and to the children.

HEALING ROOMS

Not only was God preparing Ephrata Community Church for growth in ministry within the church, but He was also continuing to stretch them as they resourced the region. As Breath of Life focused on inner healing, God began to birth a ministry focused on physical healing. After reading books about John G. Lake, an evangelist who prayed for healings in Spokane, Washington in the early 1900s, the Lord began to plant a seed in the hearts of Barry Wissler and Ken Keim for a similar ministry in the Lancaster area. Ken, pastor of Covenant Community Church, carried an urgency in his heart to see this happen and asked, "Why can't we have this now?" After all, Mark 16:17–18 confirmed, "And these signs will accompany those that believe…they will lay hands on the sick, and they will recover." (NASB) To their surprise, they discovered that Rev. Cal Pierce had reopened Lake's Healing Rooms in Washington State, so they planned a trip to observe what God was doing. Their visit confirmed that God was calling them to pursue this type of ministry. Plans were made, individuals were trained, and Ken Keim was appointed as director.

In April 2001, the Healing Rooms opened in the ECC offices, but the decision was soon made to move the ministry to Lancaster City so that it would be more accessible to the public. Because the Healing Rooms represented the whole body of Christ and not just one denomination, Ken and Barry chose a neutral site. The Healing Rooms was moved to a suite of offices and operated with approximately 20 trained people to minister in teams of three to the sick each night.

As the team depended on God and received direction from the Holy Spirit, they confirmed what specific healing was needed, laid hands on people, and often anointed them with oil. The Healing Rooms were not staffed with pastors or healing evangelists but rather with lay Christians equipped and released to pray for the sick, just as it is encouraged in the Bible. The ministry sought to work in conjunction with the medical field, not in opposition to it, and it was closely overseen by a group of pastors. The ministry acknowledged that God heals in a variety of ways, but healing is always God's work, not man's. He receives the glory.

People came from many different churches, mostly through word of mouth, to help with the ministry. The multi-church ministry had workers from 19 different churches, representing 7 denominations. With churches joining in the effort, there was power and unity, which had an effect in the healing prayer. The willingness of churches to cooperate broke down barriers and released the power of God.

THE BEST IS YET TO COME

25TH ANNIVERSARY

By October 2002, there was an excitement in the air as the church celebrated their 25th anniversary. With building plans before them and a sense that God had more in store, they were encouraged and excited to continue the journey.

Glenn Weaver, an elder, gave the church a charge: "God has been faithful with us as a church. We have gone through good times and hard times, but He has been faithful.

What drew us to be part of this church from the very beginning was that we felt that it was something that God was birthing. We knew from the beginning that there were things that He had preordained for us as a congregation to do in this area and this region. And we didn't get to do all those things yet. God uses people to accomplish His work. There is a reason He has brought you to this church. There are giftings and talents in you that God wants to use to complete and accomplish the work that He has ordained for us as a church."

Another elder, Kevin Eshleman, challenged the church: "There are people outside us, that He wants to join with us. He is going to allow our paths to cross, and they will be part of what He is doing in leading us into the future. Let's think long and let's think big. Let's think of generations beyond us and sow into that. God has called us to the harvest. It's more than the building, it's building for a spiritual harvest. The harvest field will require all of us. It's going to require whatever portion He has built into you, whatever giftings he has placed in you. It will take all of us working together for the harvest."

Ephrata Community Church was at a point where they needed to move forward and expand into what God had called them to do. Speaking to the church, Barry Wissler gave four reasons why he felt that the best was yet to come. First, the people of ECC would never accept mediocre, compla-

Barry Wissler speaks at the 25th Anniversary Banquet, October 2002.

cent Christianity. They had tasted and walked in the gifts of the Holy Spirit, and they were zealous for revival. They knew there was more to be had that God wanted to do among and through them. They loved the church and were willing to roll up their sleeves and seek God for more. Secondly, God was building a team and establishing it for the future. He had sent many leaders and prophetic people (14 of whom were former pastors) to the congregation of ECC. God had also arranged many personal contacts with national prophetic people who came to visit the

Worship Service, 2002.

church and awaken the prophetic in the region. God had anointed many with the "forerunner spirit." While God was bringing many young people, He was also bringing seasoned, mature people as spiritual fathers and mothers. Thirdly, God wanted to use ECC in the area of physical and inner healing. And fourthly, where God had once visited, He would come again. He would tear open the heavens, and the church would experience His Shekinah glory (manifest presence) together in a greater way.

Now 25 years old, Ephrata Community Church was averaging a weekly attendance of 275 people, meeting in two services each Sunday. A staff of three full-time and several part-time workers served the congregation. The eldership team was committed to building a church that continued to lead believers into active kingdom service and to reach out to those who did not know Christ. With hopes of breaking ground on the new building in 2003, they were looking forward to increased opportunities to serve the families of the surrounding community and to be a blessing to them. They were sure that the best was yet to come.

CONNECTING YOU WITH GOD AND OTHERS

A new logo and tagline were adopted in May 2003 in preparation for the groundbreaking service in September. The new logo and tagline "Connecting You with God and Others" served to strengthen and affirm the DNA of the church, which was worship and relationship with God and the building of authentic relationships with others.

Ephrata
COMMUNITY CHURCH
Connecting you with God and others

The cry of the human heart throughout culture always is to genuinely connect with God and to search for authentic community. Barry Wissler's vision for the church focused on these two things—first connecting people to

God and then connecting them to others. The tagline was more than simply a motto; it was the identity of the church. It was important for each individual to have their own personal relationship with God and to then walk in relationship with brothers and sisters in the Lord—both working together to fulfill God's plan and purposes for His body.

Along with a new tagline, a new logo was adopted depicting the Creation of Adam in Michelangelo's famous painting. The hand on the right, God's hand, was most purposeful. God had just created Adam and had released him into the garden, having complete and unhindered relationship together. In the same way, God desires for believers today to continue to seek Him and grow in personal relationship with Him. The elders believed that Ephrata Community Church needed to be a place where people could encounter and genuinely connect with God and others.

ANTIOCH REVISITED

As God was continuing to put things in place for the significant move into a new building, a definite shift was beginning to happen in God's economy and timing. The church had learned over the years that when a transition begins, those that move along with it will receive the excitement, blessings, and resources that are needed to walk it out. God was moving them forward as an apostolic resource center. In order to step into God's calling and design for Ephrata Community Church, the whole congregation needed to embrace this shift, not only the leadership. From past experience, they knew that any transition does not come easily and that they would all need to adapt and get involved.

Alan Vincent acknowledged that ECC was clearly developing into a regional apostolic center, as well as continuing to be a successful local church. An increasing number of churches and pastors were looking to Barry Wissler for input and help in their own ministries. They were finding his wisdom and non-controlling, fatherly oversight a valuable resource. Alan mentioned that in the future, a clearly defined and functioning apostolic team would need to be put in place.

Barry Wissler felt that it was time to revisit the church's call to embrace an Antioch church model. A lot had changed in the 13 years since ECC had first adopted this church model in 1990 at their family retreat. God's calling on the church, however, had not changed. And now as the shift was happening, the church needed to be reminded of what it meant to be an Antioch church.

EIGHT DEFINING CHARACTERISTICS OF THE CHURCH OF ANTIOCH

These were the eight elements of the church of Antioch that Barry felt were especially worth modeling by Ephrata Community Church:

1) ECC would need to expand its reach as a mission church in the same way Antioch reached the world by mirroring the life of Jesus Christ to others.
2) ECC would need to move beyond its race, culture, and comfort zone to take the gospel to the lost. They should not be afraid of criticism and contamination, or of bringing sinful, evil people into the church. They should be committed to godliness and righteousness, but not afraid of those not yet walking in the same manner.
3) A prominent, powerful, trumpeting prophetic gift would be crucial for the development of ECC. A personal prophetic word restores dignity, self-respect, and vision and is a crucial need of every believer.
4) A team of leaders must be in place to bring ministry balance that honors the Word of God with sound teaching and beliefs but also honors the present day truth that God speaks through His prophets and the ministry of the Holy Spirit.
5) ECC does not exist for itself and must be willing to resource some of its best leaders into missions and apostolic work for the sake of the kingdom. The new building would not be for themselves but for this purpose, the harvest.

6) ECC would be a sending and receiving church. Their mission activity must be apostolically strategized, breathed on by the Holy Spirit with the full support of the church.

7) The Holy Spirit must call the church to apostolic ministry. Prayer, worship, and fasting would provide the dynamic for continued renewal in the life of the church and would be crucial as it shifted into an apostolic ministry and resource center. The resource center would have to be built on divine guidance and not human need. The baptism of the Holy Spirit would provide the power and boldness needed for the harvest.

8) ECC was called to be a center for training and developing leaders. As their hearts were positioned rightly before God, He would pour out resources into them to impact their region and the world. ECC was a small country church, but so was Antioch, and they left a lasting impact on Christianity throughout the world.

A HEALTHY LEADERSHIP TEAM

After four years of rebuilding the leadership team, Ephrata Community Church was in a good position to move forward. At that time, Alan Vincent conducted a leadership audit for the church. He found the ECC church government to be well structured with a clear father/headship role in Barry Wissler. There was a high level of love, unity, and commitment among the elders towards Barry. The elders were loyal and working in unity under his leadership, and they possessed a solid understanding about how this delicate dynamic worked in practice. The elders were also deeply committed to the work of the church and to the leadership in the region.

Alan Vincent also found the church to have a healthy global mission interest, as well as desiring to be involved with issues of concern in the community and nation. The financial giving levels of the church were strong and managed with wisdom and integrity. The church seemed well taught in their beliefs and attitudes towards faithful and generous giving, without hype or pressure.

The sense of unity, commitment, and faith among the elders was the best it had ever been. With a healthy leadership team in place, the church felt ready and poised for the next phase of growth and purpose. Alan added only one thing for the church to consider. As ECC was moving toward an apostolic resource center and Barry would be sent out more, it would be necessary to find someone who could fulfill the role of "in house" or "home" pastor.

GROUNDBREAKING SERVICE

Finally, after years of preparation in both the physical and the spiritual realms, Ephrata Community Church held a groundbreaking service on Sunday, September 7, 2003. It was a most exhilarating time of excitement and jubilation as the church gathered under a large tent in one corporate service, along with the children, to glorify God for His faithfulness in bringing them this far.

Barry Wissler shared with the congregation that day, "We are meeting here today to give thanks to God that He's brought us to this place. Pray for the building process for 'unless the Lord builds the house we

Groundbreaking service was held in a tent, September 7, 2003.

labor in vain.' We want more than a building. We want God to fill it for Himself. It will first of all be God's house, and secondarily it will be our house, and the neighbors', and the region's. In the coming months we want to work harder to make our priority ministry to the Lord and ministry to people. That is our first priority. Not the building, but the building will be a tool that we will use to do that. This is a new day."

As each member of the building committee and Ames Construction team wore a hard hat and held a shovel, Barry read from Psalm 132:4–8. (NASB)

"I will not give sleep to my eyes
Or slumber to my eyelids,
Until I find a place for the LORD,
A dwelling place for the Mighty One of Jacob.
Behold, we heard of it in Ephrathah,
We found it in the field of Jaar.
Let us go into His dwelling place;
Let us worship at His footstool.
Arise, O LORD, to Your resting place,
You and the ark of Your strength."

Elders, building committee, and contractor break ground.
(From left: Glenn Wissler, Glenn Weaver, Kevin Eshleman, Barry Wissler, Jim Stauffer of Ames Construction, Mark Ulrich, Dale Martin, Ivan Martin), September 7, 2003.

Barry led the church in this prayer: "Father, we break ground today. We ask You to make this holy, by Your own presence. We know the land is Yours. We declare that it belongs to You. I thank You for the word this morning that You are married to the land. We thank You for this property and for what's going to happen. And we break ground, dedicating it to You and to Your kingdom. We ask You to come and fill it with Yourself, with Your presence. Use it for Your glory. And we break ground now in the mighty name of Jesus. Amen."

At the conclusion of the service, the church was encouraged to go to one of the four corners of the property for a time of corporate prayer and dedication. At the conclusion of the prayer, a shofar was blown in celebration, and the children released balloons with the church's name and information as a symbol of invitation to the world. Following the service, the church continued to celebrate with lunch and an afternoon of fellowship.

THE WELL EXPLODES

Several months later, as a group of pastors were together for a HarvestNet meeting in the barn, they heard what sounded like a loud explosion. The well drillers were digging and had hit a powerful force of water that blew the gauge and broke it. The amount of water was uncontainable, and the well had to be capped! The church leadership wondered if this could be a prophetic sign of the outpouring of the Holy Spirit to come in the future on the church and region.

BUILDING DEDICATION

Twenty-seven years earlier, a small church of 24 young adults met in a living room to discuss their vision for the future. There was a sense in the room that night that God wanted to do something very special on the property where the barn was located. Years later, as the church was preparing to move into their new building, there was still a sense of something larger to come. Prophetic words were hidden in their hearts

Steel structure being set in place, 2004.

and spirits. Ephrata Community Church began hosting a House of Prayer, with anticipation of reaching 24/7 prayer right there on the property. It was being led and attended primarily by youth from many different churches. This felt similar to the movement at the start of ECC 27 years earlier. It was still focused on worship, prayer, and relationships—but on a larger scale. God had been faithful to preserve that sense of "more" in their spirits, and now the fulfillment of that vision was visible before their eyes. After 26 years in the barn building, the church, now numbering 300, held their first worship service in the new building on Sunday, January 2, 2005. Two days earlier, they had met in the building to celebrate New Year's Eve with a time of worship and thanks to the Lord.

On January 16, 2005, the new building was dedicated to the Lord of the harvest, to the faithful Father, to their loving God. He had been so faithful and had carried them through many years of both good times and trying times. And now it was time to honor Him in the dedication of their new building. As the church entered into their new house, there were many dreams that the church wanted to see fulfilled. Barry Wissler shared ten dreams as a type of prayer.

New building was dedicated on January, 16, 2005.

10 DREAMS REGARDING THE HOUSE BUILT FOR THE LORD

1. **Let this house be a house of prayer.** Any place of worship should be a place where people can connect with God. This we will keep as our number one priority. Our new logo was created to capture this priority.

2. **Let this house be a house of His presence.** We know that God dwells in people and in the corporate body of the church. But He also manifests His presence in places that are prepared for Him and where He is welcomed. Let this building be that kind of place, where God likes to show up!

3. **Let this house be a house of friendship and fellowship.** Let it be a place where people find each other, love each other, and serve each other. A place where they desire to return to because of the atmosphere of community and belonging they experience and the connections they make.

4. **Let this house be a house full of children.** Let it be a place for them to grow up experiencing God's love and His call on their lives. Church should be children's favorite place outside the walls of their own home. God has drawn a lot of young families to ECC for a reason. So, like Jesus said, *"Let the children come unto me."*

5. **Let this house be a house that attracts youth to the Kingdom of God.** While dry and legalistic religion repels them and frustrates them, let youth find a God in this place who amazes and excites them. A God worth living for and worth dying for.

6. **Let this house be a house where generations mature and live out the fullness of their life, experiencing God through to their last days on earth.** Our dreams are not to retire and wait for heaven. We want to get *refired!* We want to be history makers. Like David, we want to serve God throughout our generation and then just go to sleep with our fathers.

7. **Let this house be a house of harvest.** We have been working out of the barn for 26 years and now we will get a *"new barn."* It will be a little bigger and a little nicer in features, but as far as bringing in the last day's harvest, it should still be a "barn" to us in our thinking. We have a whole group of new neighbors who need to hear the good news.

8. **Let this house be a house of equipping and releasing many people to live out their life purpose and destiny.** Let there be a constant calendar of training events here at ECC. Events that arrest the attention and captivate the dreams of our generation and activate them into their divine destiny.

9. **Let this house be a house of networking that multiplies connections between people and among churches in our region.** Let HarvestNet come together and let this house serve the whole Body of Christ in our region. This will not just be our house but their house, too.

10. **Let this house be a house that truly is a blessing and benefit to the people of Clay Township, Ephrata, and the surrounding region.** Any house that is built for God must ultimately be a house for people that meets their needs and adds value to their lives. It is my hope that our community will know that Ephrata Community Church loves them and is here to serve them in their hour of need.

Barry Wissler read several verses from the account of Solomon's prayer of dedication of the Temple.

II Chronicles 6:14 "O Lord, the God of Israel, there is no god like You in heaven or on earth, keeping covenant and showing lovingkindness to Your servants who walk before You with all their heart;

18-20 But will God indeed dwell with mankind on the earth? Behold, heaven and the highest heaven cannot contain You, how much less this house, which I have built. Yet have regard to the prayer of Your servant and to his supplication, O Lord my God, to listen to the cry and to the prayer which Your servant prays before You, that Your eye may be open toward this house day and night, toward the place of which You have said that You would put Your name there, to listen to the prayer which Your servant shall pray toward this place.

7:1-3, Now when Solomon had finished praying, fire came down from heaven and consumed the burnt offering and the sacrifices; and the glory of the Lord filled the house. And the priests could not enter into the house of the Lord because the glory of the Lord filled the Lord's house. And all the sons of Israel, seeing the fire come down and the glory of the Lord upon the house, bowed down on the pavement with their faces to the ground, and they worshiped and gave praise to the Lord, saying 'Truly He is good, truly His lovingkindness is everlasting.'" (NASB)

PRAYER OF DEDICATION

Barry concluded the service with a Prayer of Dedication:

"Father, I thank you for each person that came to share this time with us today. It is a special moment for us as a church. Something we have longed for and worked for and we thank You for giving this facility to us. And we today declare that this is Your house. We feel comfortable here, we feel at home. But we want You to feel comfortable and to feel at home. We want You to know how much we desperately want You. And desire You and need You. We ask You to fill this place with Your presence, Father. More than any thing else we want You to reside here and to meet with us here. We want this to be a place where people can come and connect with You and find You. And for You to change their lives, to speak to them, to bless them. And so we ask You, God, to make this place holy by manifesting Your love and Your power to all who seek You here. May it be a place where the Holy Spirit draws the lost and the hurting, the needy, and all who seek You. May it be a place that blesses this community. And we read these ten dreams into the record before You, in Your presence today asking You, God, 'Will you answer these things?' We pray that You grace us for the things that we play a part in and that we need to do. We dedicate this building, this facility, to You today in the mighty name of Jesus, giving You thanks and praise for who You are, and we ask You to use it for your purposes on the earth in the mighty name of Jesus. Amen."

During an Open House that followed, tours were given to introduce the church and the community to their new facility.

PROPHETIC WORD FROM ALAN VINCENT

In early 2005, Alan Vincent received a clear word for the church concerning the new building: "As I was coming here, I felt God clearly say to me, 'I want you to give the invitation to this church that they become a church of Thessalonica. That is, that if they fulfill the conditions that are set out in that first letter of Thessalonians, that they will become a power center for the whole region here, and it is going to be characterized by many signs and wonders and miracles, becoming a powerful house of prayer that is going to touch the whole region. And the faith of the people is going to go through the whole region. And many are going to be coming here to learn and to receive and going back to do the same in their regions.' I really believe that God has a plan of great significance for Ephrata Community Church, and we must thank God for the building. It's going to be really useful, but our passion has got to be in the vision. That it will become a regional center, a powerhouse for prayer, a place where people come to be healed, a place where we pray and shake the foundations of the demonic powers around this region so that we can see revival come all over the place. We've got to become the Thessalonica of Northeast America in Jesus' mighty name."

PRAYER: A PRIORITY

In 2004, in the midst of the building project, it became obvious that God was calling Ephrata Community Church to make prayer a priority. The first three weeks of the year were set aside for prayer and fasting. Barry Wissler shared four reasons why prayer must be a priority.

First, God had repeatedly spoken to the church about this call. A year earlier at the elders' retreat, He made it clear that the church needed to pray. Several visiting ministries confirmed the same thing, not knowing what others had already said.

Secondly, ECC expected God to suddenly pour out new wine into the church. The church needed to pray in anticipation and be ready to embrace whatever God would do. They needed flexible hearts and wineskins to be ready to receive it.

Thirdly, as they were in the midst of a building project, they were susceptible to increased spiritual warfare. Building projects can easily distract and derail a church. The church needed to stay focused on their true call—to minister to God and to others. It was important to stay vigilant in prayer during this time of distraction in all that was new.

And finally, ECC and HarvestNet had been transitioning into a greater apostolic mantel. Whenever this happens, greater warfare is sure to follow. The church needed to be strong as a base for church plantings and apostolic work in the area and to the nations. The priority in prayer rose alongside the call throughout the worldwide body of Christ to "rebuild David's Tabernacle." Rumblings were beginning to get louder, and soon the term "house of prayer" kept surfacing.

WHY A HOUSE OF PRAYER?

"Why day and night worship? Why 24/7? Because He is worthy of day and night worship and prayer to Him. We join with heaven in day and night worship to our Lord. We want an open heaven." This was the message shared by Jeff Nolt in August 2004. Jeff had taken the leadership role at Lancaster House of Prayer, which had recently transitioned out of a Bible study in the area into a more formalized house of prayer. LHOP's heart was to be a place for 24/7 worship and prayer before the Lord and a place of encounter. For Jesus said, "My house shall be called a house of prayer…" (Matthew 21:13 NASB)

Jeff felt it was strategic for the House of Prayer to move to Ephrata Community Church. They had experienced an outpouring in this place and felt there was something in the heart of God that He initiated and had planted as seed years ago. Lancaster House of Prayer wanted to join with ECC under that open heaven. LHOP's desire was to pound away at the door of heaven through prayer and worship to see His kingdom come to earth. They desired to partner with ECC in pushing through in intercession on behalf of the region.

LHOP felt there was some type of takeoff or birthing to come. A tabernacle of prayer doesn't just affect the church. It affects the entire region. As they would break through in prayer, there would be a release in the area. It was time to battle in the spiritual realm and to maintain a doorway to heaven. LHOP was positioning to become a place where individuals would come and encounter the Lord and become equipped and empowered to go out and affect the earth. In August 2004, Lancaster House of Prayer began meeting one night a week. That one night a week gathering became the seed that was sown for a continual, nonstop House of Prayer. God would water it, care for it, nurture it, and protect it. Ephrata Community Church had taken the first step toward 24/7 prayer and worship.

After ECC moved into their new building, God breathed fresh life into the old barn and slowly began transforming it into a House of Prayer. The leaders and oversight team for Lancaster House of Prayer struggled over the next year as they began to sort through, administrate, and define how a regional multi-church ministry could work together to fulfill God's call for a 24/7 House of Prayer. Like the birth of any ministry, they experienced the growing pains of coming into the actuality of God's plans for them.

HOUSE OF PRAYER HEALING ROOMS

In January 2005, after Ephrata Community Church moved into their new building, the Healing Rooms began operating alongside the House of Prayer, which was meeting in the now vacant barn. They felt the need to utilize the healing atmosphere of God's presence that day and night worship brings. The presence of God creates an atmosphere in which the sick and injured can be touched by the healing power of God. The Healing Rooms continued as a multi-church ministry with a common vision to reintroduce physical healing back into the body of Christ.

While the ministry was initially focused on physical healing, they observed while in the House of Prayer that often a physical healing was connected to a spiritual healing. The outward manifestation was an indication of something taking place inwardly. As they began to minister to the whole person, they saw more deliverances and salvations. Prophetic words flowed freely as well. When Jesus went about doing signs and wonders and the multitudes came forward, people got saved. That was the ultimate heart of the Healing Rooms—to see people freed, healed, and entering the Kingdom of God.

GATEWAY HOUSE OF PRAYER

Through leadership changes and a name change, Gateway House of Prayer was officially launched on October 25, 2005, in the Ephrata Community Church barn as a multi-church ministry. Under the leadership of Jimmy Nimon and with an oversight and planning team in place, it began functioning as a House of Prayer with a vision to cover the region in day and night worship and prayer. The hours of intercession increased as more volunteers committed to time slots.

While the Ephrata Community Church elders were in agreement with a House of Prayer in the barn, it was at an elders' retreat in the winter of 2006 that God specifically called the elders and the church

Left: Gateway House of Prayer, ca. 2007. Right: Jimmy Nimon, director of Gateway House of Prayer, ca. 2009.

into a commitment to see 24/7 prayer and worship come to fruition. The elders hired Jimmy Nimon as the full-time director of Gateway House of Prayer. With intentional purpose to establish a 24/7 House of Prayer, Jimmy developed and launched internships to train and develop worship leaders and intercessors.

In November 2008, with oversight from HarvestNet International and a multi-church board in place, Gateway House of Prayer officially reached 24/7 prayer and worship. Individuals from over 30 local churches were involved. God's calling had finally been realized. Continual prayer and worship was rising to the Lord day and night because He is worthy! Jimmy Nimon, feeling called to a new season of ministry, eventually transitioned out of the position of director, and Luke Weaver was hired to fill the role.

GATEWAY HOUSE OF PRAYER CELEBRATES 10 YEARS

As the fall of 2015 approached, the atmosphere was filled with anticipation of a celebration. It had been 10 years of God's faithfulness since Gateway House of Prayer was first launched and 7 years of 24/7 worship and prayer arising from the barn to bring glory to God!

Ephrata Community Church and the wider Gateway community

113

acknowledged that this "house" was not the idea of man but was initiated by God through multiple specific prophetic words that confirmed the prophecy in Acts 15:16–17 (NASB): "I will rebuild the Tabernacle of David which has fallen down . . . so the rest of mankind may seek the Lord." This milestone had only been possible in the context of committed community members who purposed in their hearts for this region to become a dwelling place of God in the Spirit as mentioned in Ephesians 2:22. This had come to fruition through 75,000 hours of prayer and worship, hundreds of thousands of dollars invested, and time generously given by thousands of volunteer gatekeepers and community members.

Gateway House of Prayer saw God bring significant transformation to many people, situations, and spheres of influence. But there yet remained an unfulfilled promise through a prophetic word: You are going to grow and grow in seven years, and then there is going to be an explosion of the things God is building. Worship and prayer is going to explode out of here. Together they celebrated God's faithfulness in the last season and stood in faith and declaration for the fulfillment of His purposes and multiplication for the next season. There is great expectancy for what is yet to come.

Inside the Gateway House of Prayer, ca. 2015.

REGIONAL TRANSFORMATION

As the church moved into their new building, they carried with them an excitement to fulfill their calling as a kingdom resource center. Over the years, they had heard this call through various sources. And while it had happened on a smaller scale, they were now ready to embrace it more fully in the new facility. The congregation found themselves in a good place with a team of pastors and support staff ready. HarvestNet was growing as well. The atmosphere was filled with excitement as they anticipated God's guidance in their next steps. They had dedicated the building as a resting place for God and for His glory. There was a renewed focus on the church for worship and prayer. In addition to seeing the lost saved, their greatest desire was to see the whole region transformed. Even with a new building, they could not accomplish this by themselves.

Barry Wissler began teaching that regional transformation could be possible with a shared outpouring of the Holy Spirit. The presence of the Lord was the key to the harvest. God desired to manifest His glory in a number of churches simultaneously as they partnered together. God had already been laying a foundation for this work as He began drawing several pastors and churches together. Everything in the region could be transformed by the power of Jesus Christ through prayer, partnership, and a manifestation of God's presence. Transformation would have to be God-breathed and not engineered by man.

The Lord began to turn the hearts of leaders and congregations toward their culture. God was beginning to reveal throughout the Body of Christ that culture needed to be reached through seven gates of influence: 1) religion and churches, 2) law and courts, 3) government and politics, 4) education, 5) business, 6) media and recreation, and 7) health and welfare. People would be called to work and minister in each of these gates to bring influence to the culture in these specific areas.

With the church now operating with a larger campus and a desire to transform the region, several multi-church ministries under HarvestNet's banner were birthed. In addition to Gateway House of Prayer, staffed by volunteers from over 40 churches, the Kingdom Ministry School (KMS)—originally known as the Equipping Institute—launched in the fall of 2005 to train leaders for ministry in the church and marketplace. Through their classes, KMS served over 1,400 people from over 140 churches. The Gift International was launched in 2009 to coordinate mission partnerships serving the poorest of the poor in several nations. They provided care for orphans, installed clean water systems, and fed the hungry. The faith level of Ephrata Community Church rose as they partnered with many different churches and ministries now working together for regional and global transformation

TRANSFORMATION SUMMIT

In April 2006, Ephrata Community Church and HarvestNet partnered together for a Transformation Summit. The summit was lead by Alistair Petrie, executive director of Partnership Ministries. He was joined by Ruth Ruibal, an ambassador for unity among pastors around the world, and Steve Fry, an international speaker and recording artist. Teachings on church cleansing, partnership and unity, and biblical principles of transformation strengthened a sense of corporate destiny for the region. As a representative of the public sphere, the summit was honored to host United States Senator Rick Santorum from Pennsylvania, who spoke very candidly about values, family, and the role of faith in his own life.

Between 30 to 40 churches and more than 100 pastors and leaders participated in the five-day summit, enjoying a time of encouragement and connection with each other. More than 100 intercessors prayed throughout the summit, asking God to accomplish His purposes.

Senator Rick Santorum addresses the Transformation Summit, April 2006.

A significant highlight of the summit was the Saturday night meeting during which God visibly began a work of reconciliation between

Reconciliation between the Amish and the church in the region, April 2006.

the Amish and the larger body of Christ in the region, who had functioned separately for many generations. Following a time of worship by the Amish in High German and English, a united roar of praise filled the auditorium. Singing soon gave way to tears as the Holy Spirit prompted a public expression of repentance and restoration. In brokenness, both parties acknowledged and asked forgiveness for the years of judgment and segregation, which had separated the Amish from the rest of the body of Christ. The heart cry of the Amish was clear in their repeated declaration, "We need you!"

We need one another. This was the truth that God revealed and the desire that He awakened in the regional church during the Transformation Summit. This required repentance to go deep within hearts, families, and churches within the region. There was a felt truth, recognizing that the more we seek Him, the more we find Him. As believers come to oneness in unity in the region, God will command a blessing for harvest.

GROWTH IN EVERY WAY

Ephrata Community Church continued to grow in seemingly every direction. Three years following their move into the new building, the church had doubled in size with an average Sunday morning attendance of almost 600 people. With a full meeting room and a desire to reach more people, they recognized the need for the addition of another service.

They had faith for this move as they had experienced the very same thing a few years earlier when they added a second service in the barn. The process began with building new teams of volunteers, and by September 7, 2008, they held both a Sunday morning and a Saturday night service.

God continued the amazing work of building His body at Ephrata Community Church. Streaming through the doors were people from all walks of life and backgrounds, ranging from Amish to the unchurched with little knowledge of Jesus. Stone by stone, He was building ECC—a place for everyone. During one baptism service, the Lord prompted Kevin Eshleman to ask if there was anyone else in the congregation who wanted to be baptized, making Jesus Lord of their lives. Several people responded and were baptized in their street clothes. The Lord of the harvest was working right before their eyes.

By early 2008, the opportunity arose to purchase the property adjacent to the new building, which included the Gateway House of Prayer building, an office building, and the brick farmhouse. For over 30 years, the use of the buildings had been gifted to the church rent-free and was very useful as the church had grown. Having paid off the new building in less than three years, it was an ideal time to add to the Ephrata Community Church campus.

Through these many decisions, the elders' team led the church in both their different strengths and unity of vision. The five elders used a wide variety of gifts as they served together to lead and care for Ephrata Community Church. While Barry Wissler focused on preaching and vision, each of the others held a more specialized role. Kevin Eshleman oversaw many of the teams and departments. Mark Ulrich oversaw the worship and small group ministry. Glenn Weaver was the mission's director, and Ivan Martin was the children's pastor. The team made their relationships and church vision a priority as well as the development and empowering of additional leaders. In the midst of their diversity of gifts, which brought differences of approach, the elders' team made decisions and stood together with an incredible sense of unity.

They were extremely grateful for the many others who partnered along with them in leading and serving, particularly those on the Advisory Council. These were primary ministry leaders who gave attention to a specific area of the congregational life and supported the overall vision.

ENCOUNTER YOUTH MINISTRY

A STUDENT MINISTRY PASTOR IS NEEDED

One of Ephrata Community Church's values has always been multigenerational church life, and as attendance swelled in the worship services in the years following the move to the new building, the youth group also grew. With approximately 50 teens attending the youth group meetings, the elders' desire was to see them fully engaged in God's Kingdom. As they made youth ministry a priority, they released the funding to hire a full-time student ministry pastor. After several months of searching, prayer, and discernment, Chris Weber was hired on April 6, 2009.

As Chris took the reins of youth ministry, he was humbled and grateful for those who had served before him. He mentioned the incredible legacy he inherited that was built on multiple generations of youth leaders who had served faithfully day in and day out. He was thankful for the high value they had placed on students to encounter the presence of the living God and to live in the fullness of the Holy Spirit. Growing up in the ECC youth group himself, what Chris remembered most were the stable, married couples with long-term loving

Chris Weber, Student Ministry Pastor, ca. 2015.

commitments to each other, love for God, and a committed weekly involvement with the youth.

REFLECTING BACK

It took many years for Ephrata Community Church to have an established youth group as most of the members were young couples with small children. In the early 90s, a few teens began attending ECC but had no youth group to attend. With a desire to minister to them, Dale and Jackie Martin were asked to reach out to these students, initially building relationships with them and among each other. With the few students they had, they began the hard and difficult work of laying a foundation for youth ministry in the church. On one particular retreat in 1993 with a small group of youth, guest speaker Ken Keim spoke a significant prophecy over the youth that God has fulfilled time and again at ECC.

"God says to the youth of the church—I have heard your cry, and I have called into your hearts and given you a reason for life... I have anointed you to be fruitful. I have appointed you to succeed in My Kingdom... I have given you a place in this church... I will pour out my Spirit upon you, and I will raise you up and give you purpose in your life, and I will place My favor upon you...I have called you to be those who have the stamina to run the race with endurance...I will cause you to be ones who lead the charge and who chant the battle cry... as you begin walking in these things, I will open up a thoroughfare and a highway expressway for you, and you will have opportunity to give what I've given you to your peers... the goals and purposes I have for you far exceed your dreams and your expectations, so receive the spiritual food I have prepared for you and begin where you are right now." (condensed)

Following these early years, Mark and Marlene Ulrich then carried the mantle of the youth ministry during the renewal and the following ten years. In 2005, Adrian and Janelle Kapp accepted the leadership baton for the next leg of the journey. Adrian and Janelle were very instrumental in bringing the senior high students together by initiating a weekly

Bible study for their age group. During this time, Kevin and Stephanie Eshleman also began a Bible study for the middle school students called CIA (Christians In Action). Faithful youth leaders had labored for 20 years in volunteer positions to lay a foundation, and God was building on it in this new season with the hire of a full-time youth pastor in 2009.

A LIFE INVESTED IN EPHRATA COMMUNITY CHURCH

It was a natural fit, yet designed and orchestrated by God, for Chris Weber to assume the role of student ministry pastor. Chris was born into, grew up in, married in, and started his family at Ephrata Community Church. As Chris reached his teen years, he found that he naturally gravitated to those youth on the fringes. Somewhere along the way, God had given him a real heart for those who couldn't connect. He felt wired to reach them and empathize with them. Informally, as a young adult, Chris began to meet with a group of middle school students, spending time with them and encouraging them. Eventually, he was asked to serve on the youth leadership team, which gave him more opportunity to give input into the direction of the youth ministry. He also became involved in helping with the summer kids' camp in addition to helping with the CIA group. An added incentive for his involvement in youth

Chris Weber, counselor at one of the first Kids Camps, ca. 2001.

ministry was one special young lady, Emily, who helped with the middle school students. It paid off as she later became his wife and partner in youth ministry. Emily remembers driving in the car with Chris when they were dating as teenagers, and Chris said, "I would love to work with students." Emily felt the same way as she had encountered the living God and experienced a real time of growth while she was in the youth group.

Chris humbly acknowledges that it's not just him but the team, the body of Christ working together, that provides a place for the youth to come and grow in their faith weekly. Assisting him and Emily in the first several years was a team of 9 married couples who served as youth leaders and another 22 people who served in food preparation and babysitting for the leaders' children. In 2017, an additional 6 couples were added in preparing to start a ministry to serve the 5th and 6th graders. At present, a total of 54 individuals volunteer to serve the youth of ECC. The faithfulness of these individuals has been evident as they serve the 220 students every week.

In addition to the weekly meetings, Encounter Youth Ministry continues to take the youth on annual retreats. These retreats were designed for the students to encounter the living God. Fairly common experiences include worship, times of ministry, repentance, and deliverance. Many times students are moved to tears and to celebration as their lives are being transformed in the presence of God.

Youth Retreat at North Bay, MD, 2017.

THEIR MISSION FIELD

With a desire to offer the students opportunities to engage their faith on a practical level right where they are living, Chris connected the youth with the Ephrata Project. This is a weeklong multi-church camp, serving as a local service project and involving six other youth groups. Through this project, Chris' desire has been for the students to understand that God placed them right where they were for His purposes. Their mission field is where they live and the people in their community. Many lives have been touched in the community as the students served people in need by painting, doing yard work, power washing homes, doing minimal carpentry, etc. Traveling a bit farther, they took a mission trip to Jackson, Mississippi in 2016, partnering with Amy Lancaster of We Will Go Ministries, where they learned the importance of preparing for their work each day with two hours of prayer and worship.

Many seeds were sown over the years for the youth, and not only through the youth leaders. Many guest speakers at Ephrata Community Church would address the young people specifically, often stopping in the midst of their message to speak to them. The engagement of the students drew the speakers in, and they were offered many words of blessing, encouragement, and motivation. Since the very start of the youth ministry at ECC, students have grown in their spiritual lives with a genuine desire to follow God, realizing that they had the same fullness of the Holy Spirit as any adult in the congregation.

HOLY SPIRIT BOLDNESS

One hallmark of youth group nights has been the testimony time each week. The students encourage one another to embrace the power of the Holy Spirit with boldness as they share their stories of taking Christ to the community. The testimonies of the senior high students often motivate the middle school students. A typical type of testimony was of one student who shared that a teacher in her public school mentioned in several classes that she wasn't feeling well. Two students from Ephrata Community Church prayed for her separately in two different classes, not knowing that the other one had also prayed for her. Students have

Many youth shared testimonies during their services, 2017.

often taken prayer into their schools. As God directs them, they pray, and their classmates have seen healings and the power of God. One student even brought the whole track team from Ephrata High School to Gateway House of Prayer so that he could show them what it looks like to encounter the presence of God. The intercessors at Gateway prayed and prophesied over the whole team. These are just a few of the countless testimonies heard on a regular basis in the student ministry.

As students reach out to friends, they bring them to their meetings. On any given night, there are at least ten visitors, some of whom show up without knowing anybody. The meetings have been rich with visitors. Chris Weber observes that at some point there was a significant shift towards evangelism among the youth, but he isn't exactly sure when it happened. As a result of this growth within the youth group, the elders hired Joel Bomberger in 2016 as a resource evangelist for the youth to assist in fueling them towards the work of evangelism.

Chris' core message to the students continues to be that you cannot work your way towards goodness or righteousness. Rather, it is only through belief in Jesus Christ and putting on His righteousness that allows anyone to connect with God. Chris is continually reminding the youth that they do not need to strive to be "good enough" and that their standing with God has nothing to do with their behavior. God just loves them, wants to meet them, and will do the work of changing their hearts and lives as they obey Him in loving others in their schools, families, and community.

WORSHIP LOVERS WITH PASSIONATE HEARTS FOR EVANGELISM

Presently in 2017, Chris and Emily acknowledge two things that stand out among the youth of Ephrata Community Church. First, they love to worship God without reserve. There is an abundance of talented, skilled, and creative worship leaders with a calling to pioneer worship training in leading others into genuine worship. With this desire and their God-given skill, they have written many of their own worship songs. Second, as previously mentioned, they have passionate hearts for evangelism.

Chris and his team take no credit for what God had done among the youth. Many times, the leaders stand in awe and are challenged by the testimonies coming from the students. It is an experience bigger than any one of them. They are reaping what others had sown as they watch their faithful God moving in the lives of the teens.

As the ministry continues to grow, Chris' vision is to see the influence of the students continue to expand in their schools as they pray for

Passionate hearts worshipped God at a retreat, ca. 2016.

those around them in need. He sees the awareness of God raised, not because it is in the textbooks, or because they are allowed to pray, but rather because their hearts have been changed by the presence of God and they believe He can do the same for their friends. It's the life of Christ present in the school in a very real and tangible way.

Chris Weber recently shared, "There is a whole generation of young people who are growing up with a superficial understanding of Jesus. They may have had some basic Christian teachings, they may have heard the name of Jesus, or possibly even grew up in our churches. Unfortunately, they have never encountered the living Christ, His power over sin and death, and the presence of His Holy Spirit in their lives. As a result of this "words without power Christianity," they have become absolute cynics, and they have no interest in religion. A similar story is told in John 1:43-48 as Nathanael, a young man at the time, responds cynically to Philip's question of whether or not Jesus could be the Messiah. Philip's invitation of "come and see" is the same invitation that we give to young people today. When Nathanael finally meets Jesus, Jesus gives him a simple word of knowledge concerning who Nathanael is and what is going on in his life. As a result Nathanael responds, 'Teacher, you are the son of God, King of Israel!' There is a whole generation of young people waiting to encounter the living Christ, and when they do, they will be hooked for life. That is the vision I have for this generation—authentic encounters with the living Jesus Christ."

REALIGNING TO GOD'S PURPOSES

With a thriving youth ministry in place and the church growing exponentially, the first several years in the new building seemed like a whirlwind. The leadership team was busy caring for all the new people God was sending their way, while also hosting regional events. Barry Wissler felt God calling the church to align once again with His purposes as He prepared the church for the things to come. The values below were given to provide clarity of purpose during a busy season of growth for the church and to prepare them for the change yet to come.

12 VALUES OF EPHRATA COMMUNITY CHURCH

1. ECC values facilitating, embracing, and entering the Kingdom of God, the domain over which God rules, in our lives corporately and individually. ECC exists for God and to give Him glory, for the chief end of man is to love Him and enjoy Him forever. ECC wants to be a place where God manifests His presence and to corporately serve and love Him through our submission and obedience. The rule and reign of God affects every area of our lives.

2. ECC values the recognition of the Holy Spirit as a person and as God and must be worshiped and honored just like the Father and Son. ECC's desire is that each person experience the Holy Spirit personally, a gift that was given to us. One of ECC's goals is to introduce each member to the Holy Spirit. ECC expects revivals and outpourings of the Holy Spirit repeatedly and increasingly, with intensity. The church lives in the age of the Spirit birthed by Pentecost.

3. ECC values multigenerational ministry. There is value in generations publicly worshipping God together. Teams are encouraged to work together in the church ministries. The older must turn their hearts to the younger, and the younger must respect the older to receive their blessing. Each generation is needed and valued.

4. ECC values obedience to the Great Commission by taking the Gospel to the lost and making disciples "as you go" in life. Whatever is learned, whatever is received is reproduced in other people. ECC exists for the purpose of populating heaven at hell's expense. ECC's job is to rescue others, making disciples and teaching everything that Jesus taught.

5. ECC values the restoration of apostolic ministry and teamwork. The apostolic is the catalyst for the restoration of the five-fold ministries. The apostolic creates breakthrough and advancement by getting people to work together. Apostles make sure that the foundations of the church are accurate and truthful, keeping the church focused and moving forward.

6. ECC values building authentic community. Community is real life flowing between people happening outside of the Sunday morning service. The church is a family, not an event; a group you belong to, not a place you attend.

7. ECC values 24/7 prayer and the Tabernacle of David, a power-house manifestation of God's presence marked by extravagant worship and passionate intercession. God's people, young and old, coming together in extravagant worship to seek His face and give themselves only to Him. The Tabernacle of David is not just for intimacy but a place carrying the warrior spirit to fight the wars and battles and the demonic forces in our region. Through worship and prayer, the spiritual atmosphere is changed.

8. ECC values the restoration of signs and wonders as God's King-dom comes. Through prayer and with active faith, we become participants in restoring signs and wonders, which will increase as they are taken to the lost.

9. ECC values commitment to a life of stewardship. They hold what they have as if it belongs to God, giving to those in need with compassion. They never lose by giving.

10. ECC values commitment to the unity of the Body of Christ. As the Holy Spirit brings unity, the church desires to maintain it through forgiveness and forbearance and partnering with other churches.

11. ECC values community transformation and is dedicated to serving the culture and finding favor within the culture. The church chooses to be a friend to the culture, influencing and seasoning it with the salt and light of their Lord.

12. ECC values participation in the labor and rewards of a great harvest. The church will stay heavily invested in reaching the unreached in the United States and in other nations. This is reflected in their spending and budget.

THRESHOLD CHURCH

With church planting always at the forefront of their mission, Ephrata Community Church was excited and honored to help prepare a group of believers to plant a church in Lancaster city. Jeff Nolt and Cory Martin had gathered a core group with the intention of planting a church. The great commission was at the center of their mission with a desire to reach the city. Recognizing the anointing and calling of God on them, the leadership of ECC and HarvestNet offered support in launching the new congregation. ECC graciously offered them an eight-month internship with the elders in preparation for the church plant. This involved a combination of learning opportunities, ministry experiences, and responsibilities designed to prepare them to lead the church.

On February 8, 2009, Ephrata Community Church and Harvest-Net commissioned Jeff Nolt as senior pastor and Cory Martin as an elder of Threshold Church. The ECC elders and the HarvestNet board laid hands on them and prayed over them in a sending service. With HarvestNet as the credentialing organization and ECC as the supportive church, Threshold set out with 55 adults and a number of children. It was an exciting day of celebration as ECC continued to come into their destiny as a sending, Antioch-type church.

ELDER ORDINATION

As the church continued to grow, the Lord raised up two men to help the other five elders shoulder the responsibilities of leading and caring for

Jared Bruckhart and Jon Chappell ordained as elders (Seated from left: Mindi & Jared Bruckhart, Jon and Joanna Chappell), October 24, 2010.

the congregation. For the previous decade, the church had thrived and received God's blessing under the unity of the eldership team. This unity in turn flowed down to the church body as a whole. It was important to the leadership team that any others added to them would walk in the same manner of unity and submission to one another.

Through a process of seeking the Lord and discernment, Jared Bruckhart and Jon Chappell were ordained as elders on October 24, 2010. Both men consistently modeled the kind of character and integrity that Scripture sets forth for leaders. Their wives, Mindi Bruckhart and Joanna Chappell, joined with their husbands as they supported them in the work of leading and caring for the people of Ephrata Community Church in the next season.

PROPHETIC AFFIRMATION

The first six years in the new building were, at times, a whirlwind of God's movement through the church as it was growing and expanding in all areas. Over the years, God had faithfully sent prophets and advisors to speak into the church. November 2011 was yet another of those times. Jim Goll, a prophet who ministered internationally, visited ECC and gave a prophetic word that would affirm the church in the direction they were going and the vision before them.

Jim Goll prophesied, "I saw two words written out in the Spirit over this particular house. I saw the word 'faithfulness' and I saw the words 'progressive vision'… You have been enormously faithful. Faithfulness is your outstanding characteristic and Jesus has a reward system in the Gospels for faithfulness. Jesus is the one who taught if you are faithful in little, He will make you faithful over much. And if you are faithful in natural mammon, He will make you ruler over true spiritual riches. That is God's reward system, and it's God's reward system over this apostolic center that is arising for such a time as this.

It is faithfulness, but it is faithfulness mixed with progressive vision. A lot of people are faithful. They are stuck and they are stewards of yesterday, and get this, they are a parked car in a cul-de-sac sitting in the car acting like they are going somewhere, and they are not. But you have faithfulness and progressive vision. I declare that you are mighty; I declare you are victorious in Christ Jesus. I say that worship, worship, worship is one of your greatest strengths.

I say one of the reasons why this is an apostolic center is that barn over there. You never vacated your barn, you maintained the little manger. You've never gotten too big in your attitude because God always uses 'little ol' me's.' He always gives grand jobs to those who see themselves small in their own eyes and see God great. I speak a blessing over this house of faithfulness, and I speak a blessing of ongoing, continuing apostolic, prophetic, progressive vision. I speak a blessing that you shall be part of the courageous army that arises: the army of light in this hour that helps to write the continuous chapter in the book of the war of the Lord for such a time as this!" (condensed)

ADDITIONAL LAND PURCHASE

As the church continued to grow at an unexpected rate, it became apparent that they should consider purchasing additional land along

Route 322, which was owned by Ephrata Community Hospital. The hospital was willing to sell three lots to the church after placing a five-year contingency on them. In 2011, with the purchase of extra land, the church now felt confident that they had the necessary land to fulfill God's calling for the church on the campus on Clay School Road.

SPEAKER OF THE HOUSE—NEWT GINGRICH

In April 2012, one highlight in the midst of everyday church life was the opportunity for the leaders of Ephrata Community Church and HarvestNet to host the former Speaker of the House and presidential candidate, Newt Gingrich. He was accompanied by his security detail for a special meeting with church, business, and community leaders. Gingrich challenged those present to remember their Christian heritage in America and encouraged them to be bold in their public stand for Jesus Christ. He expressed the need to cultivate the atmosphere for another Great Awakening. The visit was a reminder to the leadership to continue pursuing their primary call to influence the culture around them.

Former Speaker of the House and presidential candidate, Newt Gingrich, addressed HarvestNet, April 2012.

PASSING THE BATON
2014 – 2017

ACTS 13 MOMENT

Looking at the history of the church, it is clear that Ephrata Community Church was genetically designed for growth. It was in the church's DNA from the start. The New Testament church as described in Acts 2:42–47 was the pattern by which ECC was built, including strong community and apostolic teaching. The Acts church broke bread together as a symbol of their continual dependence on the death of Jesus Christ. Prayer was a primary focus as a means for intimacy with God. Miracles and the supernatural were evident, along with their care for the needy amongst them and in the community. They had large temple meetings and smaller home meetings. They continually praised and worshipped God. Any church with this foundation in place would grow, as did ECC.

The church had experienced a shift in the mid 80s, focusing outward towards missions and more fully adopting the Antioch model for church life. The church at Antioch was a receiving church but also a sending church. Acts 13 speaks of the "setting apart" and "releasing " of Barnabas and Paul for the work to which they were called. Ephrata Community Church was approaching an Acts 13 moment of sending. God was calling Barry Wissler to invest more time in the work of building within HarvestNet and other areas in His kingdom. The elders stood with Barry as he felt called to transition in giving the remainder of his life and ministry to developing and training leaders both locally and internationally. This was not an easy decision as Barry and Cheryl and the church had enjoyed the love, unity, and peace of the eldership team that God had established. But they also recognized that sometimes healthy teams have to release healthy team members to further God's purposes. ECC was facing their Acts 13 moment. If Ephrata Community Church was indeed modeling the Antioch church, this would be a test of their releasing ability.

As Barry was being called to minister more and more outside of ECC, he noticed that his grace for ECC was shifting as well. God's grace was always sufficient, but His grace and focus seemed to be moving towards different things. This change prompted the need to find someone whose focus would be on the local "home" congregation. Barry noticed that God had been increasing Kevin Eshleman's vision and grace for the local church. In 2007, several years before any official change in leadership would happen, Barry casually asked Kevin if he might be interested and willing to become the senior pastor at some point in the future. Although Barry wasn't sure when it might happen, he felt that the time would come.

APPROACHING THE MOMENT

By August 2012, Barry and the elders began a 3–5 year transition process to move Kevin and the church through a carefully-orchestrated transfer of the senior pastor position. Kevin and his wife, Stephanie, had processed the decision through prayer together as a couple and sought direction along with the elders and leaders. Advisors Alan Vincent and Marc Dupont also confirmed the transfer of Kevin into the role. Other confirmations had come through prophetic words from Jim Goll and a Kenyan church apostle.

To prepare Kevin for the role of senior pastor, God guided Barry to Numbers 27:15-23. Moses put some of his authority on Joshua so

Barry Wissler and Kevin Eshleman.

that the people would learn to obey him. Moses had not left his God-given post immediately, but he began to step back into a more fatherly oversight role. In the same way, Barry began to slowly give Kevin responsibilities and over time learned that he could always count on Kevin. He was continually willing to sacrifice and step up to meet the needs of the congregation. When Barry would leave on a ministry trip, Kevin would assume his role, and when Barry returned, Kevin would step down. Kevin's commitment revealed his willingness to lay his life down for the flock, a necessary attribute for a senior pastor. God had given him a heart for the sheep of ECC and a heart for the community, and the church's trust in Kevin deepened. It was a sign that God was placing a mantle on Kevin to lead the church and giving him the plan and blueprint for the future.

Barry had led the church with an apostolic anointing and was now preparing to hand the church over to Kevin, who also walked in a similar apostolic anointing. With the Antioch nature of Ephrata Community Church, it was necessary for another leader to carry the same gifting and vision. Kevin was connected to other nations as well as many churches and ministries in the region. Other pastors responded to Kevin as a mentor and advisor to them in their own ministries.

FAITHFUL FOUNDERS

God established Ephrata Community Church, but in building it up, He had also raised up a leader to lead the congregation. For 37 years, Barry Wissler faithfully served as senior pastor, and his wife, Cheryl, had served right alongside of him. In many ways, their difficult job was to lay a foundation on which others could build.

Barry had provided the congregation with leadership that had been consistent and firm but without control, which was a very hard balance to maintain. He provided direction to the congregation that was rooted in the authentic integrity of the Scriptures, while at the same time opened the door to the work of the Holy Spirit and the unusual ways in which God sometimes works. It was a difficult balance to lead a church in, but it was accomplished under Barry's leadership. He preached the standard and the truth as a shepherd of the flock, while also extending grace to all in need outside of the congregation.

Barry Wissler was authentic, consistent, and lived his life with integrity. This was his character, and it showed in every aspect of his life. Barry carried significant wisdom and could speak into church situations or structures, bringing clarity and helping countless people. He was instrumental in offering a word of wisdom at just the right time so that others might avoid heartache and trouble in their own ministries. He had a way of training up and multiplying leaders, making a way for them in the church and calling them into their place at ECC. Barry possessed a faith to believe God against all odds simply because He trusted God to be who He said that He is and that through Him all things are possible.

Barry and Cheryl Wissler, 2014.

Barry and Cheryl would not be leaving Ephrata Community Church. The church would be their home base as they ministered around the world. This was a very unusual and significant pastoral transition in that Barry and Cheryl would remain in the congregation at ECC. The church was thrilled that ECC would still be their home. For Barry, it was important for him to have a local church home. He believed the local church, with Jesus Christ as the head, was the hope of the world. ECC was his home, his family, and he loved it. He had enjoyed his life and work within ECC and acknowledged that God was good to him and Cheryl in this place.

With Barry Wissler still connected to ECC, the church could fully embrace the partnership they had with HarvestNet International as well. It would keep them engaged as a resource church, which was written into their DNA and mission. As a local church in the village of Clay, they had the privilege and opportunity of ministering all over the world through Barry and Cheryl and HarvestNet International. This was an incredible honor for the congregation. HNI and ECC would benefit from each other; their health and their sustenance would come from one another.

Barry and Cheryl paid a high price for the "house" of ECC. Romans 12:1 simply says that—in view of God's great mercy, offer yourselves as a living sacrifice, as holy and pleasing to Him, which is your spiritual act of worship. And that is how Barry and Cheryl viewed that verse. They wouldn't say that they did anything outstanding, but they simply believed that in view of who God is and all that He's done, how could they have done anything less?

BARRY'S FINAL CHARGE TO ECC AS SENIOR PASTOR

Barry shared some final thoughts as he left his role as senior pastor. He reminded the church of the three questions that David asked his mighty men in 1 Chronicles 12:17.

1) Have you come in peace?
2) Have you come to help me?
3) Will you let your heart be joined to mine?

Barry requested the church to apply those questions to Kevin. He asked them to join their hearts to Kevin—to serve him, pray for him, and protect him—and that it would be a joy for Kevin to lead the church.

As the church would embrace what God was going to do, they would need to release some things in order for the church to grow. Barry Wissler reminded the congregation that there were some things Ephrata Community Church would never lose. The key to fruit and fulfilling God's will and plan for the life of the church was to know what to let go of and what to cling to. Because Kevin Eshleman had been with ECC for many years and with the eldership team remaining the same, there wouldn't be big changes at first. But eventually some change would come with a new vision caster and carrier, and God would give Kevin pieces to add and things to tweak. This transfer would allow God to take ECC to a new level of effectiveness in reaching unbelievers in the community and in impacting the nations.

One thing Ephrata Community Church would cling to was something from their very inception. Twelve people met together and said, "I think God is calling us to be a church." In that moment, in that place, there was a heart and passion to know God in the power of the Holy Spirit, through Jesus Christ, and make Him known to others. It was just really that simple. At the very heart of it, at the very core, was a passion to simply know God. Knowing God and making Him known to others would carry through to the next senior pastor and the next leg of the journey for the church.

GOD DIRECTS KEVIN ESHLEMAN TO THE CHURCH

Kevin and Stephanie Eshleman had begun their married life as farmers, raising beef livestock in Mt. Joy. Many times they would drive on Clay School Road and were intrigued by the barn with the name Ephrata Community Church across the front. In 1992, they bought a farm in

West Cocalico Township and moved into the area. Weekly, as they drove to their church in Mt. Joy, they would again pass the barn, thinking that they should go sometime. One day Kevin pulled into the parking lot, checked out the service times, and decided that the following Sunday they would attend Ephrata Community Church.

During that week, a bishop in the Brethren in Christ church showed up at Kevin's house and asked if he would consider a call to the ministry in the BIC church. Even though they were heading directly to ECC, God simply took them in another direction for several years. Initially, Kevin had been pretty resistant to the idea of going into ministry, but God made it clear to him that it was His will, and Kevin was licensed for ministry in 1992 in the BIC church. Kevin began pastoring and taking some foundational Bible courses during which time God was dealing with some areas of his life. While he was willing to obey God on the outside, there was much resistance on the inside. In the midst of his inward struggles, he was also struggling to balance pastoring and farming. In addition, his family had grown to include two toddlers, Hannah and Daniel. He began to hear stories about different things that God was doing in meetings at ECC, but with his farming responsibilities, there was no time to get away.

One evening as Kevin was reading the Lancaster Newspaper, he noticed an article on the front page, reporting that God was doing something very special and unique at Ephrata Community Church. Stephanie, knowing the state Kevin was in, said, "You're going. Aren't you?" And he replied, "Yes, I am." That evening, not trusting to bring his wife yet, Kevin went to observe and investigate what God was doing. He left the meeting with all kinds of questions as to what was happening, but God simply let him know that it was Him. Kevin returned the following week. God met him and literally in a moment brought transformation and renewal. All the things weighing him down were suddenly gone in a very astounding way.

In 1998, the Eshlemans sold the farm and left the BIC pastorate

Kevin and Stephanie Eshleman, 2002.

for ministry with the Lancaster Youth for Christ—later known as Lancaster Youth Network of Churches (LYNC)—as a public school campus minister. Later that year, they began attending Ephrata Community Church, followed by a time of uncertainty about whether this was indeed the place for them. But God answered clearly, "No, this is where I have you. You stay and just serve." So they joined the church and gave their hearts to serve the congregation. It wasn't long afterward that they began to lead a home group, and in 1999, Kevin was ordained as an elder. As his position with Lancaster Youth Network of Churches was decreasing, Barry Wissler and the elders made it clear that they desired for his work with ECC to increase.

Beginning in 2003, Kevin Eshleman began working one day a week in the ECC office. Within a year, his employment became half time. By 2005, he came on full time as executive pastor. In preparation for his calling from God, Kevin studied and obtained a master's diploma from the Wagner Leadership Institute and a Master of Divinity in World Christianity at Evangelical Theological Seminary in Myerstown, Pennsylvania.

As God was moving Barry Wissler into an apostolic calling to the nations, He was faithfully nurturing and caring for Kevin Eshleman and moving him into position to lead Ephrata Community Church into a new season. God was looking for a leader He could trust to lead this church and one who would guard the DNA He had created in them. He found that leader in Kevin Eshleman.

INSTALLATION OF KEVIN ESHLEMAN

Following an overwhelming confirmation vote from the congregation

Elders install Kevin Eshleman as senior pastor, November 23, 2014.

and a seamless transition, the time had come to make the official transfer of the senior pastor role. It was time to finalize the Acts 13 moment. On November 23, 2014, Kevin Eshleman was officially installed as the senior pastor of Ephrata Community Church. As Barry Wissler and the elders prayed and laid hands on Kevin, with Stephanie by his side, the congregation stood in support as they participated in installing their new senior pastor. Barry commented, "I consider what's happened to us to be a real work of God. I am happy to finish and I am happy to pass this to Kevin. The word God gave me for this church was that the 'glory of the latter house will be greater than the former.'"

Barry addressed Kevin personally, "One more thing I need to do. I need to give you this church. It is important to release this church to you and your leadership. I give you the shepherd's staff. A shepherd's staff is a symbol of the shepherd leading the flock, protecting the flock, caring for the flock. This was given to me a number of years ago. It says *Ephrata Community Church* on it. So as a symbol of what we are doing tonight, I give you this church, and with that, I give you this staff." And so the baton was passed, the staff was passed, and the Acts 13 moment was completed.

Barry Wissler gives the shepherd's staff to Kevin Eshleman, November 23, 2014.

KEVIN ESHLEMAN, SENIOR PASTOR

Addressing the congregation for the first time as their new senior pastor, Kevin Eshleman thanked the congregation for their hunger for the Lord that had pushed the leadership to make Ephrata Community Church a place that would not settle for mediocrity but would press forward to receive what God had for them. Kevin thanked the eldership team, whom he had served alongside for 15 years. It was an amazing team, not an "I" team. They led together, supporting and standing with each other.

Kevin said, "I accept this calling to care for you as the reflection that Jesus Christ is the good shepherd and to give you the required leadership in all the aspects of congregation life in this place. And I commit to you today before the Lord to be strong and courageous in leadership, to hold to the Word of God as our final authority, to live the Word, to preach the Word, knowing that God will provide everything that I need for this role and that we need together as a congregation to run the race that is marked before us. With God's help and by His grace, we will hit the mark. We will fulfill the plan that He has for us for His glory. And I will and we will not fear, for God is with us."

Kevin continued, "I appreciate your support, and it truly is a privilege to serve the congregation of Ephrata Community Church. You have a heart that just loves God and pursues the Lord. We want the reality of God and all that He has for us here. In preparation for this time, I feel like the Lord has given me 12 things that He has called me to declare over this congregation that will be a part of our future. I will refer to Ephrata Community Church but, as you know, that's you, not the building. This building is only a building; it's only a tool for us to meet in. So when I refer to the house and I refer to Ephrata Community Church, it's us, the people of Ephrata Community Church."

12 DECLARATIONS FOR EPHRATA COMMUNITY CHURCH

1. **This house will be a house of Worship.** May Ephrata Community Church be a people of authentic worship; may we reflect the desire of our Father who seeks for those who worship in spirit and in truth. May God give us new ways to express our worship using all the arts and all that we are to give Him glory.

2. **This house will be a house of Prayer.** May Ephrata Community Church be a people of prayer, expressing our humility before the Lord and our dependence on the Lord, reflecting His desire that His house is to be a house of prayer.

3. **This house will be a house of His Presence.** May Ephrata Community Church express the heart of Moses in Exodus 33 and refuse to settle for anything less than the manifest presence of God, knowing that it is His presence that distinguishes His people from all the people of earth.

4. **This house will be a house of Discipleship.** May Ephrata Community Church be a people whose lives are transformed by the renewing of our minds. May all of us be living, breathing

testimonies of the transforming power of God, so that our light might shine before men, giving praise to our Father in heaven. Just like the believers at Antioch, may we so reflect our Savior that we are labeled with Him.

5. **This house will be a house for Children.** May Ephrata Community Church have lots of children as we reflect the heart of Jesus who said, "Let the little children come for to such is the Kingdom of heaven." May we receive children and may we be a people that encourages and equips future generations for all that God has for them.

6. **This house will be a house for Youth.** May Ephrata Community Church be a place where youth find purpose and direction; a life worth living for the glory of God.

7. **This house will be a house for all Generations**. May Ephrata Community Church be a people where all generations grow together, work together, and advance the Kingdom together.

8. **This house will be a house of Harvest.** In Matthew 9 Jesus expresses a shortage of harvesters for a plentiful harvest. Jesus, we respond by saying, "Here are we, send us!" Ephrata Community Church will be your witness in Jerusalem, Judea, Samaria, and the remotest part of the earth. Jesus was accused of being the "friend of sinners." We willingly receive the same label. May this be a place where sinners find hope, restoration, redemption, and a new life in Jesus Christ.

9. **This house will be a house of Generosity.** May Ephrata Community Church be a people of generosity, knowing that we, as a congregation, do not exist for simply our own benefit, but for the benefit of others. Freely we have received, freely we will give, wherever we can, however we can.

10. **This house will be a house of Community.** The reality of our relationship with Jesus Christ is lived out in relationship with others. May Ephrata Community Church be a people of authentic community.

11. **This house will honor all in the Body of Christ.** We acknowledge the body of Christ is large and diverse, and we choose to honor all expressions of the church of Jesus Christ while living out our specific role in the body.

12. **This house will be a house of His Glory.** May Ephrata Community Church be a place where our Lord Jesus Christ receives all the honor and glory that is due His Name.

A new season for Ephrata Community Church had begun. But one thing had not changed; it was ultimately for God and His Kingdom. It was all for His glory. Everything that was done and said during the transition service was committed into His hands and acknowledged that He was in the midst of it. It was only because of God's faithful hand that Ephrata Community Church was in the place they were. It would be only through Him that they would be able to move forward. Just as they had trusted Him in the past, they would trust Him for the future, for His character never changes. He was faithful. He had always been faithful, and they had no doubt that He would always be faithful. It was their declaration that His kingdom would come and His will would be done on earth as it is in heaven.

LIFEWAY CHURCH PLANT

As the elders began discussing the possible expansion of their current building in 2014, Jimmy Nimon, director of Gateway House of Prayer, along with his wife, Lydia, approached them with a passion in their hearts to plant a church. After a season of prayer and discernment, Kevin Eshleman and the elders felt it was an authentic call that God was placing on Jimmy and Lydia at this time. God had entrusted Ephrata Community Church with His message and the desire to share it with

ECC elders installed Jimmy Nimon as pastor of Lifeway Church, August 8, 2015.

as many people as possible. The elders felt God calling them to pursue both an expansion of their current building and to support this church plant. ECC was in a good place and the congregation was comfortable, strong, and healthy. With another church plant on the horizon, the elders chose once again not to be comfortable, but rather to stretch themselves and the church for the sake of the Kingdom.

During the next several years, Jimmy Nimon joined the staff of ECC in a type of internship as he made the necessary preparations. He connected with a church-planting ministry, Association of Related Churches (ARC) that became a valuable resource. On August 8, 2015, Ephrata Community Church launched Lifeway Church. Kevin Eshleman and the eldership team prayed and laid hands on Jimmy and Lydia, blessing and commissioning them for the work God was calling them to in Lebanon County, Pennsylvania. Feeling the call of God on their lives to join the church plant, a team of about 90 people was commissioned with them.

Ephrata Community Church is honored to partner with Lifeway Church for the advancement of the Kingdom. They are committed to Lifeway's success by offering ongoing financial, administrative, and leadership support for the next several years.

MINISTRY FACILITY EXPANSION

As ECC continued to grow in number under the leadership of Kevin Eshleman, the three weekend services began filling up again. It became necessary for Kevin and the elders to turn their attention to the possibility of expanding the current building.

In December 2015, Kevin began casting a vision to the congregation for a building expansion during a message entitled "Love Looks Like Something." He said, "We haven't been chosen to be stored up someplace and kept away, but we have actually been chosen to demonstrate Jesus. Jesus said, 'You didn't choose me, but I chose you and appointed you that you should go and bear fruit' (John 15:16 ESV). So we are chosen for a purpose. And the purpose is that while we are living on this earth we are to demonstrate who Jesus is to the world around us.... We want you to take a look at your community with the eyes of Christ and say, 'How do I incarnate Christ in the place where he has put me?'" Kevin challenged each individual to find their calling in the community and to get involved in meeting needs.

Kevin shared that while individuals were called to serve the community, the corporate body had the same calling. Expanding the building would need to serve the community and change lives for eternity, a priority and value of Ephrata Community Church. Years earlier when the congregation had moved into their new building, some were unsure about leaving the barn. They loved the barn and had a history in it. The Holy Spirit had met them there. They had spent a

"Community Center" signage on barn, 1979.

147

lot of time on the floor in the presence of God. He had spoken clearly to them in the barn. Moving from the barn to the huge new building had been unsettling as they processed what it would be like in a new place of worship. But ECC would not have grown if they had stayed in the barn. Once again, the elders recognized that to remain confined in their current church building would limit growth, and that was unacceptable. God's priority was for the harvest and the lost in the community, and so it had to be their priority as well. Church would never be just about ECC, but also a passion to reach the lost and make space for them. Forty years earlier, God's heart for the lost in the community had been planted as a seed into the heart of the church where He had faithfully watered it and preserved it. The first words on the barn in 1978, "Community Center" were a testament to that initial seed.

With their priority focused on a building that would also serve the community, the elders began to dream and make plans for the new expansion. A knowledgeable building team was put in place to navigate all the aspects of a large building project. A financial team began strategizing for project funding. The elders' faith ran high as they remembered God's faithful provision through their last building project and property acquisitions. Each of the previous debts had been paid off in less than three years. The church was debt-free once again and held a reserve. The leadership was committed to executing the project without shackling the congregation with a large debt that would financially inhibit the ministry of the church.

Together, the elders, the building team, and the finance team began the process of answering the call to build a ministry facility expansion. They envisioned the auditorium holding community events such as concerts, recitals, school district programs, etc. as well as smaller spaces being made available for business, educational, and recreational usage for all ages. The plans included a large café with an indoor play area for children that would be open during the week for the community. The possibilities were endless, but all were considered with a focus and passion to see the lost saved and the region transformed.

STAFFING FOR MINISTRY

As Ephrata Community Church obeyed the call to be a "sending" church, Kevin Eshleman found himself in a position with a diminished pastoral staff. Three of his six pastors were being sent out; Barry Wissler to lead HarvestNet International, Jimmy Nimon and Jesse Rothacker to plant Lifeway Church. The remaining pastoral staff was Kevin Eshleman, Mark Ulrich, and Chris Weber. This became a testing point for the leadership as the congregation numbered 1,100 people in an average week and was growing rapidly. In addition to the decrease in pastoral staff, two of the administrative staff were also sent out to help with the Lifeway Church plant.

At one point during all of the staffing changes, Kevin sat in his office, crying out to God for answers. In that moment he heard God say, "Hang tight and I will bring you the people you need. Do what I ask of you and things will come into order." Kevin responded with a simple faith response of "Okay", and along with it came a strong sense of confidence, which he imparted to the remaining staff as he asked them to hang in there along with him. There was agreement that everything was going to be okay, and they would get through it.

God further instructed Kevin Eshleman that as change was coming, it needed to be purposeful change. God was faithful in showing Kevin that he needed to rebuild, not because the previous staff had been bad but because there was going to be a launching out. The change coming was about more than bringing Ephrata Community Church up to where it needed to be. It was equally about preparation for the future. Kevin began to talk to the elders about staffing specifically for ministry. Adding to the skeleton staff became an ideal opportunity to step back and to rebuild for the purpose of pastoral care, followed by the administration to support it. As they focused on staffing, God began building a team. The team that God joined to Kevin and the elders was far better than they could have imagined or assembled on their own.

INSTALLATION AND COMMISSIONING OF THE PASTORAL TEAM

By early 2016, four pastors had joined the Ephrata Community Church pastoral team. The team, now numbering seven, was built together neither for self-recognition nor for the recognition of Ephrata Community Church. God built the team with the purpose of glorifying Jesus Christ and all that He wanted to do through the ongoing ministry of ECC.

As God identified leaders and brought the team together, there was an overwhelming sense that He had something more in store for the congregation. Kevin Eshleman stated, "I can stand here and say that I wasn't twisting arms to get people on staff, but it was a God thing in what He is doing and accomplishing here, and it's pretty amazing."

As the pastoral team was installed and commissioned, Kevin charged them with God's commissioning to Joshua found in the first chapter of Joshua:

"Do you fully embrace the responsibility and call to serve as an ambassador of Jesus Christ in your specific area of ministry calling as well as a team together? Do you accept the calling that God has placed on you to incarnate the reality of Jesus Christ to this congregation and to serve this congregation for the purposes of equipping for the work of ministry, for the building up of the body of Christ, for the unity of the faith, for knowledge, for the revelation of Jesus Christ, and for maturity? And do you commit this day before the Lord and this congregation to be strong and courageous in leadership, to hold to the Word of God as the final authority, to live the Word, to teach, preach, and demonstrate the Word, knowing that God will always be with you and will always provide everything that is required for fruitfulness and success so that you can fulfill all that God has intended for you and for this congregation. If so, indicate by saying that you will."

The pastoral team members installed and commissioned together as a team were:
Kevin Eshleman—Lead Pastor

Neil Beatty—Pastor of Children's Ministry
Beverly DeRise—Associate Pastor of Children's Ministry
Dennis Scalese—Pastor of Administration and Pastoral Care
Wes Siegrist—Pastor of Discipleship and Global Missions
Matt Swords—Pastor of Discipleship and Young Adults
Mark Ulrich—Pastor of Worship and Pastoral Care
Chris Weber—Pastor of Student Ministry

GOD JOINS MORE STAFF TO THE TEAM

With a strong pastoral base in place, God provided additional administrative staff to support the pastors added to the team. Kevin Eshleman and the elders rejoiced and thanked God once again for His faithfulness in providing a team to support the work of the church. While the elders felt that they had added enough staff to accomplish the vision of God for the church, God surprised them by introducing three additional staff to the leadership. These were in the areas of missions, worship, and prayer—all three of which were strong in the DNA of the church from its earliest days. God was clearly interested in taking them to a new level in these areas of ministry. The church had placed emphasis on all three areas in the past, but God seemed to be setting things up for an expansion or multiplication.

MISSIONS

Eight months after Wes Siegrist was hired as Pastor of Discipleship and Global Missions, God sovereignly brought a mission consultant to assist him in developing a sustainable missions program that could support the growth of missions at Ephrata Community Church. Jim Ehrman, a dean at Evangelical Seminary, came with extensive experience in international and global ministries, relationships with international churches, and relief and development work in several nations. Bringing Wes and Jim together with their skills was a great partnership. Wes had years of local church and pastoral experience, with a calling to evangelizing the unreached and to teaching and discipling believers. Jim, with his missiology background, introduced a broad organizational approach to missions along with many global connections.

Haiti, 2005.

Guatemala, 2009.

India, July 2017.

Ephrata Community Church had always valued its outreach to the nations, beginning with their first mission trip to Guyana, South America, in 1983. Many short-term teams were added here and there over the years that followed. Most of the mission contacts were through HarvestNet International, which had brought the local church and international partnerships together with their shared values and purposes. While missions had expanded considerably, it was not sustainable for the growing church. With a broad involvement spread thin over many areas, it was time to evaluate their focus points in missions.

Wes and Jim began the task of wrestling through God's vision and plan for Ephrata Community Church in building the missions ministry. They recognized that God had placed skills in the hands of the congregation for a purpose and a plan both locally and internationally. Wes and Jim's desire was to connect each person in the congregation in some way to the work of missions.

Wes Siegrist was reminded of the missional heartbeat of Ephrata Community Church when over 80 people attended the initial mission's interest meeting. The desire within the group was not only for global missions, but also to serve the Lord wherever He called them. It was yet more evidence that the seed God had planted in the 12 individuals in a living room in 1977 had produced fruit, which now reached 13 nations and supported 20 local partnerships. But there was more growth and fruit yet to come. While carefully holding and honoring the already-present missions legacy and with the Holy Spirit as their guide, Wes and Jim began the process of building a sustainable model for missions, which would take Ephrata Community Church into the next season.

WORSHIP

Worship was important in the birth of Ephrata Community Church and its history. During significant seasons when God was moving in unique ways, worship was always at the center of connecting the congregation with the palpable presence of God. Mark Ulrich, an elder, led the worship for over 40 years, even before ECC officially became a church. His heart burned with a passion to connect with God's Spirit in worship, where power could flow from His Spirit and touch people as they encountered the presence of God.

Mark Ulrich had laid a foundation for simple, passionate worship to God, while raising up a multi-generational worship team that consisted of 35 musicians and vocalists that rotated on a monthly basis. A support team of sound and lighting technicians assisted in providing and setting the atmosphere. Through the years, Mark realized that as a

Worship team, late 1970s.

true apostolic resource church, there was a need to build, grow, and develop the musical creativity, gifts, and resources that God had richly deposited in the church.

Once again, God sovereignly brought Donnie Kittle as a teammate to assist Mark in the purpose of developing the worship ministry. Donnie was hired in early 2017 as Director of Music Ministry, bringing with him 37 years of music ministry experience. Mark Ulrich sensed that Donnie's gifts could help develop and channel the creativity planted within Ephrata Community Church. Isaiah confirmed what was in Mark's heart as Donnie joined the team, "Enlarge the place of your tent, and let the curtains of your habitations be stretched out; do not hold back; lengthen your cords and strengthen your stakes." (Isaiah 54:2 ESV)

Mark and Donnie knew in their spirits that Ephrata Community Church was sitting on a well of creativity. Original music that was capturing the "now heart" of God for the church and the region was already being written and produced. Their desire was to seek out the giftings and creativity sovereignly given to ECC for the advancement of His Kingdom. Many budding worship leaders, songwriters, and musicians were emerging, all with the purpose of fulfilling the mission of ECC as a resourcing church. Presently, only several months into 2017, there are already visions and discussions about summer music camps, a music ministry school, individual music lessons, a recording studio, along with many other proposed plans. Mark and Donnie are pursuing this partnership in response to a belief that God wants to do something in Ephrata Community Church to release fresh creativity that will impact culture as it touches the community, region, and the nations.

PRAYER

While Gateway House of Prayer had been operating in the barn on the campus of Ephrata Community Church for over ten years, it was a multi-church ministry overseen by HarvestNet International. Though launched from ECC, HarvestNet had developed into more of an international ministry. With Gateway being a regional house of prayer, the timing seemed right to move the oversight of Gateway from HarvestNet International to the elders of Ephrata Community Church.

Therefore, in January 2017, Ephrata Community Church took full responsibility for the Gateway House of Prayer, not as ECC's house of prayer but as a multi-church house of prayer established, motivated, supported, and resourced by ECC for the sake of the entire region. Along with this organizational transition, Luke Weaver, the director of Gateway House of Prayer, and his staff joined the staff of Ephrata Community Church. As Luke and his family were called into a season of ministry training, a shift in leadership was on the horizon. On August 29, 2017, a transition service was held signifying the shift in leadership from Luke Weaver to Bonita Keener. The service was a celebration of the past and an affirmation of God's leadership into the future of the Gateway House of Prayer.

VISION WEEKEND

With new team players in place, it was evident that God was preparing the church for a new season, and excitement rose within the church. To bring renewed focus and align-ment, Kevin Eshleman set aside a weekend of services in January 2017 to examine God's call and vision for Ephrata Community Church. Kevin challenged the church, "that with God all things are possible. When we think about God and who He is, there are no limitations. They are all gone!" Referring to 1 Corinthians 2:9, Kevin stated, "Your eyes have not seen what God has planned for you. Things may seem beyond our

Kevin Eshleman, ca. 2016.

reach, but that is what we are going to do. Reach beyond ourselves for all that God has for us."

ECC'S FULFILLMENT OF AN ANTIOCH CHURCH

During the Vision Weekend, Kevin Eshleman reminded the congregation of the Antioch church model upon which the elders and staff had built Ephrata Community Church. The weekend was a time of building faith and vision in the church body for the future. Kevin addressed the following seven aspects of the Antioch church model as related to ECC.

1) **A church that welcomes everyone**
   a. Everyone is welcome at ECC.
   b. Not only the individuals on the platform, but everyone at ECC creates an environment where people can be received.
      i. ECC has asked for 500 commitments to Jesus Christ for 2017 either through their services or ministry flowing out of the congregation.
      ii. It is not the goal of ECC to be a large congregation. The goal is to properly steward what God has given them. They make adjustments for those God sends to them. With almost 1,300 people attending each weekend, a fourth service will be added in September 2017.
      iii. In addition to the weekly services, ECC welcomed an online presence of 560 views each week, many from other countries.

2) **A church where they are called Christians** (A term used first in Antioch given by society because they lived like "little Christs")
   a. ECC is called to live out the truth of who Jesus Christ is and to respond. Not mere hearers but doers as well. The real test of ECC begins Monday morning as they live out their Christianity.
   b. The congregation is encouraged to "Take One Step."

     i. Groups—Each person is encouraged to get involved in one of the many types of small groups.

    ii. Message Notes provided in the Worship Guide assist the church in walking out what is taught.

3) **A church that does both "receiving and sending"**

    a. ECC received various gifts brought by five-fold ministers visiting from throughout the Body of Christ. These individuals, filled with grace and anointing, inspired, motivated, and imparted something to the congregation.

    b. ECC has been a sending or releasing church. "A church is not measured by its seating capacity but by its releasing capacity." (as quoted by Glory Dhas of India) ECC has released and sent out the following:

        i. Barry Wissler—HarvestNet International

       ii. Threshold Church in Lancaster City

      iii. Lifeway Church in Lebanon County

      iv. Short-term mission teams and long-term missionaries

4) **A Church that is generous**

    a. As freely as ECC has received, they have also given.

    b. Missions Giving—25% of tithes and offerings went to missions outside of ECC. In 2016, $406,000 was given to missions locally, nationally, and internationally. Additionally, 71 individuals gave of their time and finances to go on five mission trips to four nations.

    c. Apostolic Resource Center

        i. ECC will take responsibility and care for their region.

           1. Gateway House of Prayer—a multi-church house of prayer covering the entire region in prayer

           2. Music and Worship

Ministry—developing and resourcing the region through possible summer camps, music schools, etc.

3. Building Expansion—ECC is not building a building for themselves but for the community. It's a venue where they can serve their community.

4. Association of Related Churches (ARC) ECC is a partner with ARC, a church-planting network, in planting churches as well as receiving help from them.

5) A Church full of faith

a. The gospel of Jesus Christ is what the world needs. Within the three counties surrounding ECC, Berks, Lancaster, and Lebanon, no less than 500,000 people live without any church connection. ECC is not content to live in a region where ½ million people are living without any type of security in Christ. They believe that God has entrusted the answer to the world's problem to them because Jesus is THE answer.

b. ECC knows they cannot do it on their own. They will partner with other congregations in the Body of Christ across the region and do their part. They know, without a doubt, this is what God is calling them to do.

c. ECC desires to see more healings, signs, and wonders.

6) A Church of teamwork

As the saying goes, "Teamwork makes the dream work." Kevin Eshleman says, "What you see around here has far exceeded my leadership ability. God is doing an amazing work. It's Him doing the work. What happens around here happens because there is a teamwork atmosphere involved."

   i. Elders Team—Seven couples
  ii. Pastoral Care Team
 iii. Discipleship Team
 iv. Local and Global Missions Team
  v. Children and Youth Team
 vi. Worship Ministry Team
vii. Creative Team
viii. Gateway House of Prayer
 ix. Administrative Team
  x. Other Teams—Volunteer Teams
     1. Hospitality Teams
     2. Ministry Teams
     3. Outreach
 xi. 500+ volunteers
     1. Serving over 300 hours/week of volunteer time.

A VERY SPECIAL SEASON

At the start of 2017, Ephrata Community Church entered into a very special season. The year ahead provided them the opportunity to reflect over the past 40 years of their time together and of God's faithfulness. As they looked forward from this point, they stood confidently on their experience of Him and full of faith for the future. With a potential ministry facility expansion in the near future, countless hours had been spent designing and planning a building that would best serve the congregation and God's work in their midst.

The expansion being planned would have a three-fold purpose. 1) It would provide a place where ECC could better minister to the needs of the community. The community would be a primary focus in consideration of the design and use of the building. 2) It would meet the needs of the growing congregation. The facility would provide the space needed for ministry to youth, children, and the larger congregation.

3) It would help the congregation establish a stronger base of ministry, enabling them to reach other areas of the region through church planting and supporting ministries.

After much research and discernment in considering both congregational needs and capacity, the eldership team of Ephrata Community Church determined that a facility project within the framework of 15 million dollars would best suit the church's needs for ministry expansion. In June 2017, the congregation cast their votes in accordance with the church's bylaws. After prayerful consideration by the congregation, the elders received an overwhelming 96% "yes" vote to move forward with building the new facility. With affirmation from the congregation, the eldership team along with the building teams continued to pursue God's plans and purposes for the new expansion.

Presently, a 40th year anniversary celebration is being planned for Sunday, October 22, 2017. As the church plans its 40-year celebration, they remember with amazement the long journey that God has taken them on from their humble beginnings to the place of expansion they are in today. Standing on assurance of His faithfulness to them in the past, they will continue to honor Him with faith for the future as they look forward with anticipation to His leading and guiding.

Projected ministry facility expansion.

FOR SUCH A TIME AS THIS

When reflecting upon the whole story of Ephrata Community Church up to this point in time, it can almost be compared to the story of Esther in the Old Testament. God took a group of teenagers and faithfully raised them up as the congregation of Ephrata Community Church for such a time as this. ECC has become a special place only because the grace of God rested on them through the years. Time and time again, His grace motivated them to pray, press in, and recognize that He had more for them. It was always about Him and what He desired to do in and through them. In every change or addition to ministry or program, their commitment was always to support God's movement. They remained committed to ensuring that no program was ever held as more sacred than what He was doing. They strived as a body to remain adaptable as they followed His lead so that they could always make way for the Holy Spirit to work through them in changing lives and bringing transformation.

Lead Pastor Kevin Eshleman reminds the congregation regularly that ultimately it is about people meeting Jesus Christ. The Lord Jesus entrusted ECC with a message – the message that Jesus Christ transforms lives. Because of sin, people are separated from their heavenly Father, and the church has been given the incredible opportunity to reunite them in love and relationship with their Father. The highest goal and achievement of Ephrata Community Church must always be to give God the glory. It's never been about ECC as a church, and it can never be about them if God's purposes are to be fulfilled. ECC exists for His glory, and that must always be their posture and their aim.

While the history of Ephrata Community Church reveals a great foundation, God's continued faithfulness promises an even greater future. Programs, ministries, and systems can be put in place. But, like in seasons past, it will be only through the power of the Holy Spirit that Ephrata Community Church will be launched into fullness in the next 40 years. As they move forward, ECC holds to the promise of God in Ephesians, "Now to Him who is able to do immeasurably more than all we ask or imagine, according to His power that is at work within us, to Him be glory in the church and in Christ Jesus throughout all generations for ever and ever! Amen." Ephesians 3:20-21 NIV)

TIMELINE

1977 October 16	First meeting of 12 people in a living room.
1978 March	Members begin to convert a barn into a youth center.
1979 Spring	First Sunday morning service meets in barn.
1981 April 1	Barry Wissler installed as pastor.
1981 October 2	Ray Ciervo and Edification Ministries network begins a relationship with the church.
1982 April	Weekly home groups established geographically.
1982 July	Church attends first Summer Conference with Edification Ministries.
1983 October	First missions trip to Guyana, South America.
1984 September 25–29	First community outreach at Ephrata Fair stand selling shoofly pie and ice cream
1985 April 17	Ephrata Community Church adopted as new name replacing Servants of Love Community Church.
1987 December 12	Mark Ulrich ordained as elder.
1988 January 4	Clay After School Program opens in church basement.
1990 April 12-14	First Spring Family Retreat at Black Rock Retreat Center
	Church adopts Antioch church model.
1990 Spring	Office building renovated for the church and New Covenant Ministries.
1990 June 2 & 3	Leon Price introduces the church to the prophetic.

1993	Mission statement adopted: Proclaiming the Gospel, Producing Disciples, Preparing Workers, Planting Churches.
1993 March 21	Ken Keim ordained as elder.
1994 April 17	Covenant Community Church launched.
1994 July	Renewal begins with an outpouring of the Holy Spirit.
1995	Emphasis on prayer begins.
1995 September 19	School of the Spirit begins with emphasis on Bible study and training.
1996 May 24 & 25	Sixty men from ECC go to Promise Keepers Conference in Washington D.C.
1996 September 9-14	River of Life meetings with Randy Clark.
1997 March 22	Church services moved to DOVE Christian Fellowship facility on Saturday nights.
1997 October 14	Elijah House Video School starts.
1997 October 18	Willow Street Community Church and
1997	Boanerges Christian Fellowship planted.
1997 December	Church services moved back to the barn.
1998 March	Elijah House Video School graduates 56.
1998 October	Breath of Life Ministries begins.
1998 October 24-26	Alan Vincent speaks for first time to the church.
1999	Alan Vincent's relationship with Barry Wissler and ECC is defined.
1999 June 6	Kevin Eshleman, Ivan Martin, and Glenn Weaver ordained as elders.
1999 October 31	Marc Dupont gives prophetic word, "If you build it, they will come."
2003 July	"Connecting you with God and Others" tagline adopted.
2003 September 7	Groundbreaking ceremony held in tent for new church building.
2004 August 10	Lancaster House of Prayer meets at ECC in an effort to build a 24/7 House of Prayer for the region.

TIMELINE

2004 December 31	First event in the new building, New Year's Eve party.
2005 January 2	First service in the new building.
2005 January 11	Healing Rooms opens in conjunction with the Lancaster House of Prayer.
2005 October	Gateway House of Prayer launched in barn.
2006 April 20-24	Transformation Conference hosted with HarvestNet.
2008 March 28	Farmhouse, Gateway barn, and office building purchased and added to campus.
2009 February 8	Threshold Church commissioned through ECC and HarvestNet.
2010 February 11-14	First missions conference hosted by ECC in partnership with HarvestNet.
2010 October 23 & 24	Jared Bruckhart and Jon Chappell ordained as elders.
2011 August	Building lots along Route 322 purchased for future use
2013 September	Contracted with Cornerstone Design to design a ministry facility expansion.
2014 November 23	Pastoral Transition Service. Kevin Eshleman installed as senior pastor. Barry Wissler to direct HarvestNet International.
2015 August 15 & 16	Lifeway Church commissioned and launched
2015 October	Gateway House of Prayer celebrates 10 years of worship and prayer and 7 years of 24/7 worship and prayer.
2017 September 9 & 10	Fourth weekend service added.
2017 October 22	40th year anniversary celebration.

12 DECLARATIONS FOR EPHRATA COMMUNITY CHURCH SCRIPTURE REFERENCES FROM PAGE 143

1. This house will be a house of Worship.
   a. John 4:23–24

2. This house will be a house of Prayer.
   a. Matthew 21:13
   b. Isaiah 56:7

3. This house will be a house of His Presence.
   a. Exodus 33:15–17

4. This house will be a house of Discipleship.
   a. Romans 12:2

5. This house will be a house for Children.
   a. Matthew 19:13–15

6. This house will be a house for Youth.
   a. Ecclesiastes 12:1

7. This house will be a house for all Generations.
   a. Psalm 148:12–13
   b. Joel 2:28–29

8. This house will be a house of Harvest.
   a. Matthew 9:37–38
   b. Luke 15:1–2

9. This house will be a house of Generosity.
   a. Matthew 10:8

10. This house will be a house of Community.
    a. Psalm 68:4-6

11. This house will honor all in the Body of Christ.
    a. 1 Corinthians 12:12–14

12. This house will be a house of His Glory.
    a. Ephesians 3:20–21